Meredith Zinner

Bruce Norris

CLYBOURNE PARK

Bruce Norris is the author of the play *Clybourne Park*, which had its world premiere at Playwrights Horizons Mainstage Theater and was also produced at the Royal Court Theatre. It won the 2011 Pulitzer Prize for Drama, the 2011 Laurence Olivier Award for Best New Play, the 2010 London Critics Circle Award for Best New Play, and the 2010 Evening Standard Theatre Award for Best Play. His other plays include *The Infidel* (2000), *Purple Heart* (2002), *We All Went Down to Amsterdam* (2003), *The Pain and the Itch* (2004), and *The Unmentionables* (2006), all of which had their premieres at Steppenwolf Theatre, Chicago. His newest play, titled *A Parallelogram*, premiered there in July 2010. His work has also been seen at Playwrights Horizons (New York), Lookingglass Theatre (Chicago), Philadelphia Theatre Company, Woolly Mammoth Theatre (Washington, D.C.), Staatstheater Mainz (Germany), and the Galway Festival (Ireland), among others. He is the recipient of the Steinberg Playwright Award (2009) and the Whiting Foundation Prize for Drama (2006), as well as two Joseph Jefferson Awards (Chicago) for Best New Work. As an actor he can be seen in the films *A Civil Action* and *The Sixth Sense*, and in the recent *All Good Things*. He lives in New York.

CLYBOURNE PARK

CLYBOURNE PARK

Bruce Norris

Farrar, Straus and Giroux

New York

Farrar, Straus and Giroux
18 West 18th Street, New York 10011

Copyright © 2011 by Bruce Norris
All rights reserved
Printed in the United States of America
Originally published in 2011 by Nick Hern Books, Great Britain
Published in the United States by Farrar, Straus and Giroux
First American edition, 2011

Library of Congress Control Number: 2011931149
ISBN: 978-0-86547-868-8

Designed by Emily Kent

www.fsgbooks.com

21   20

For Frances Watson

CLYBOURNE PARK

By Bruce Norris
Directed by Pam MacKinnon

World Premiere
Playwrights Horizons Mainstage Theater
Opening Night: February 21, 2010

The cast was as follows
(in order of speaking):

ACT I (1959)

Bev	Christina Kirk
Russ	Frank Wood
Francine	Crystal A. Dickinson
Jim	Brendan Griffin
Albert	Damon Gupton
Karl	Jeremy Shamos
Betsy	Annie Parisse

ACT II (2009)

Tom/Kenneth	Brendan Griffin
Lindsey	Annie Parisse
Steve	Jeremy Shamos
Kathy	Christina Kirk
Kevin	Damon Gupton
Lena	Crystal A. Dickinson
Dan	Frank Wood

TIME AND PLACE

The set is the interior of a modest three-bedroom bungalow, 406 Clybourne Street, in the near northwest of central Chicago. There is a sitting room with front door access, a fireplace with an oak mantelpiece, and a separate dining area with built-in cupboards. At the rear of the dining area a swinging door leads to a kitchen. A staircase leads up to a second floor, and beneath it, another door leads down to a basement. There is a hallway and a bathroom door as well.

CHARACTERS

ACT I (1959)

RUSS .... white, late 40's

BEV ....married to RUSS... white, 40's

FRANCINE.. black, 30's

JIM .... white, late 20's

ALBERT ....married to FRANCINE .... black, 30's

KARL .... white, 30's

BETSY................married to KARL ....late 20's

ACT II (2009)

TOM *(PLAYED BY THE ACTOR WHO PLAYED)*... JIM

LINDSEY .... BETSY

KATHY...BEV

STEVE ....married to LINDSEY ....KARL

LENA .... FRANCINE

KEVIN ....married to LENA ....ALBERT

DAN ....RUSS

KENNETH .... JIM

Note: In the original production, the actor playing Jim and Tom also played the role of Kenneth. In some subsequent productions a separate actor was hired to play the role of Kenneth alone.

Act I

*(September 1959. Three o'clock, Saturday afternoon. The house is in
disarray. Cardboard boxes are stacked in corners. Some furniture has
been removed, shelves emptied. Pictures have been removed from the
walls and carpets have been rolled and stood on end. Not far from the
fireplace, RUSS sits alone reading a copy of National Geographic.
He is dressed in pajama top and chinos, socks, no shoes. On a table
next to him sits a carton of ice cream into which, from time to time,
he dips a spoon. Music plays softly on a radio next to him.)*

*(After some time, BEV descends the stairs carrying linens to place in
a cardboard box. As she packs, she stops to look at RUSS.)*

BEV

You're not going to eat all of that, are you?

(He turns down the radio.)

RUSS
(with his mouth full)

Whaddya say?

BEV

What ice cream is that?

RUSS

Um. *(Looks at the carton.)* Neapolitan.

BEV

Well, don't feel compelled to eat that.

RUSS
(shrugs, barely audible)

Going to waste.

*(He turns the radio back up and FRANCINE enters from the
kitchen, wearing a maid's uniform. RUSS remains in the foreground
as BEV joins her.)*

FRANCINE

(to BEV)

So, if it's all right I'm just going to put these candlesticks here in the big box with the utensils.

BEV

That is what I would do, yes, but you do mean to wrap them first?

FRANCINE

Oh, Yes ma'am.

BEV

Oh. Now: Francine: I was wondering about this chafing dish, which we have practically never used.

FRANCINE

Yes ma'am.

BEV

Do you own one of these yourself?

FRANCINE

No, I sure don't.

BEV

Because I do love to entertain though for the life of me I can't remember the last time we did. But still, it does seem a shame to give it away because it's just such a nice thing, isn't it?

FRANCINE

Oh, yes it is.

BEV

And it's just looks so lonely sitting there in the cupboard *so*: I was wondering if this might be the sort of thing that would be useful to you?

FRANCINE

Ohhhh, thank you, I couldn't take that.

                                BEV
                          (re: chafing dish)
See how sad he looks?

                              FRANCINE
You don't want to be giving that to me.

                                BEV
Well, nonetheless I'm offering.

                              FRANCINE
No, I don't think I should.

                                BEV
Well, you think about it.

                              FRANCINE
But thank you for offering.

                                BEV
You think about it and let me know.

                              FRANCINE
Yes ma'am.

                                BEV
And do put some paper around those.

                              FRANCINE
Yes ma'am.

        (FRANCINE goes into kitchen. BEV continues packing, passing
        RUSS as she crosses.)

                                BEV
That's a funny word, isn't it? Neapolitan.

                                RUSS
                          (turns off radio)
Funny what way?

BEV

What do you suppose is the origin of that?

RUSS

Uhhh… Naples, I imagine.

BEV

Naples?

RUSS

City of Naples?

BEV

Noooo.

RUSS

Of or pertaining to.

BEV

That would not be my first guess.

RUSS

Yup.

BEV

I would think it had something to do with *neo,* as in something *new,* and then there's the *–politan* part which to me would suggest a *city,* like *metropolitan.*

RUSS

Could be.

BEV

Meaning *new city* or something to that effect.

RUSS
(shrugs)

Told you what *I* think.

BEV

Because a person from Naples, I mean they wouldn't be called, well, not *Napoleon*, obviously. I guess that was already taken! *(laughs, then serious)* On the other hand, you *do* say *Italian*. But *cities*, though, and specifically ones that end in *S*, because there must be a rule of some sort, don't you think? Help me think of a city other than *Naples* that also ends in S?

(Pause.)

RUSS

Uhhh –

BEV

Oh fiddle. Um.

RUSS

Des Moines.

BEV

Not a *silent* S.

RUSS

Brussels.

BEV

All right. There you go. And how do we refer to them?

RUSS

Belgians.

BEV

But, the people from the *city*.

RUSS

Never *met* anyone from Brussels.

BEV

But there has to be a word.

RUSS

Look it up.

BEV

Where?

RUSS

Dictionary?

BEV

But it's not going to say this is the capital of Belgium and by the way the people who live there are called —

RUSS

Give Sally a call.

BEV

She won't know that.

RUSS

She and Ray went to Paris.

BEV

So?

RUSS

Close to Brussels.

BEV

Sally never knows those sort of things.

RUSS

Oh. Oh.

BEV

What?

RUSS

Parisians.

BEV

What about them?

(FRANCINE returns with more packing.)

RUSS

Paris ends in S.

BEV

But – It's not *Brusselsians.*

RUSS

Or Nice.

BEV

I'm serious.

RUSS

Got the "S" *sound.*

BEV

But not *Nicians.* Like *Grecians.*

RUSS

No, no. *Niçoise.*

BEV

I know that, but –

RUSS

Know that salad your sister makes?

BEV

But that's *French.*

RUSS

It's a French *city.*

BEV

I understand, but, I'm saying how would we say, in *Eng*– ? Well, now I don't remember the original question.

RUSS

Brussels.

BEV

No no.

RUSS

Des Moines?

BEV

No.

RUSS

Naples.

BEV

Naples. And I don't think *Neopolitan.* How would that become *Neopolitan?*

RUSS

Muscovites.

BEV

What?

RUSS

People from Moscow.

BEV

Well, I give up, because that's just *peculiar.*

RUSS
(*chuckles at the word*)
Muscovites.

BEV
(the same)

I wonder if they're *musky.*

RUSS
(savoring the sound)

 Musss-covites.

BEV
(coming up with one)

Cairenes!

RUSS

That is a strange one.

BEV

I'm telling you, that's what they're called!

RUSS

I'm not disputing.

BEV

But why *Cairenes?*

RUSS
(shrugs)

Dated a girl named *Irene.*

> *(FRANCINE exits again.)*

BEV

Or *Congolese?*

RUSS

That, too, is correct.

BEV

So why don't we say *Tongalese?*

                        RUSS

Or *Mongolese.*

                        BEV

No, Mongol-*oid.*

                        RUSS

No no, that's different.

                        BEV
                (embarrassed)
Oh, you're right.

                        RUSS

That's uhhh, you know, that's –

                        BEV

No, I know.

                        RUSS
        (tapping his finger on his temple)
The thing with the –

                        BEV
                (doing the same)
Like the Wheeler boy.

                        RUSS

Right. The one who –

                        BEV

Bags the groceries.

                        RUSS

Right.

                        BEV
                (beat, then:)
But that's nice, isn't it, in a way? To know we all have our place.

                    RUSS
There but for the grace of God.

                    BEV
Exactly.

          (Pause. RUSS breaks it with:)

                    RUSS
          (pronouncing grandly, with a sweep of his hand)
Ulan Bator!

                    BEV
What?

                    RUSS
          (an exact repeat)
Ulan Bator!

                    BEV
What are you doing?

                    RUSS
          (once again)
Ulan – !

                    BEV
Stop it. Tell me what you're doing.

                    RUSS
Capital of Mongolia.

                    BEV
Well, why would I know that?

                    RUSS
          (shrugs)
National Geographic.

BEV

Oh, oh . . . Did you change the address like I asked you?

RUSS

What do you mean?

BEV

For the *National Geographic.*

RUSS

The address?

BEV

Oh, *Russ!*

RUSS

Me?

BEV

I *asked* you.

RUSS

You did?

BEV

I asked you *fifteen times.*

RUSS

When?

BEV

I said don't forget the change of address for the magazine and you
promised me that you would, you promised me *specifically* – *(cont'd.)*

RUSS
(overlapping)

I did it last week.

BEV
(continuous)

– that you would see to it so I – Oh.

RUSS

Pulling your leg.

BEV

I see.

RUSS
(a gentle imitation)

Oh *Russ!!*

BEV

Maybe people don't *like* having their leg pulled.

RUSS

I was just – I was – Okay.

(Pause.)

BEV

And are you going to bring that trunk down from upstairs?

RUSS

Yup.

BEV

Thought you said after lunch.

RUSS

Sort a two-person job.

BEV

And you really want to wear those clothes all day?

RUSS

Hadn't really thought about it.

(A silence passes between them. RUSS scratches his elbow.)

BEV

But you know, you *are* a funny person. I was telling Francine – I ran
into Barbara Buckley at Lewis and Coker's and Barbara said that
Newland told her a funny joke that you told at Rotary last year.

RUSS

That *I* told?

BEV

About a man with a talking dog?

RUSS
(shakes his head)

Thinking of Don Lassiter.

BEV

No, It was you.

RUSS

Don's the one with the jokes.

BEV

You know jokes. You tell jokes.

RUSS

A talking *dog?*

BEV

And Barbara said does Russ not go to Rotary anymore? Apparently
they all keep saying where's Russ? *(a beat, then)* Not that I care one way
or the other but it does seem that you used to enjoy going and I don't
see why that, of all things, should have to change – *(cont'd.)*

(RUSS shifts in his chair.)

BEV
(continuous, quickly)

– and please don't say *what's the point*, Russ. I hate it when you say that. Because for that matter – *(cont'd.)*

RUSS
(overlapping)

I wasn't going to say –

BEV
(continuous)

– what's the point of *anything* enjoyable, really? – *(cont'd.)*

(Phone rings. FRANCINE enters.)

BEV
(continuous)

– Why not just sit in a chair all day and wait for the end of the world but *I* don't intend to live the remainder of my life like that and I think you could take notice of the fact that talking that way *frightens* me.

FRANCINE
(answering phone)

Stoller residence?

RUSS
(quietly, to BEV)

Not trying to frighten you.

FRANCINE

Who may I say is calling, please?

RUSS
(to BEV, quietly)

Ulan Bator!

FRANCINE

Excuse me, Miz Stoller?

BEV

Who is it?

FRANCINE

Mister Lindner wanting to talk to you.

RUSS
(with a groan)

Ohh for the love of –

BEV
(to FRANCINE)

Tell him I'll call him back.

RUSS

Not one thing it's another.

FRANCINE
(phone)

Mister Linder, she wonders if she can call you back?

BEV
(overlapping FRANCINE, to RUSS)

I only mean that people are concerned about you – *(cont'd.)*

RUSS
(overlapping)

Well, what's the *nature* of the concern?

BEV
(continuous)

– and I don't see the point of *spurning* their good intentions.

RUSS

Gee whiz I'm just reading a magazine.

FRANCINE
(to BEV)

Says he's calling from a pay phone.

RUSS
(to FRANCINE)
Just say we're occupied.

BEV
No, I'll take it, thank you Francine.

(to RUSS, as she crosses)
I'm just repeating what Barbara said.

(into phone)
Hello?

RUSS
(to himself)
Barely know the woman.

BEV
(phone)
No no no, it's just, we're in a state of disarray, Karl.

RUSS
Somehow I *spurned* her.

(As FRANCINE returns to the kitchen, the front door opens and JIM sticks his head in. He is a youthful minister — wears a clerical collar under his jacket.)

JIM
Ding-dong?

RUSS
(seeing JIM, not rising)
Oh. Uh, hey, Bev?

JIM
May one intrude, he politely asked?

                                RUSS
                            (to BEV)

Jim's at the door.

                                BEV
                (seeing JIM, she mouths silently to him)
Oh, oh, oh! *Come in!! Come in!!*

                            (into phone)
Karl, I can't hear what you're saying.

                                JIM

Russ, my friend, I am crossing the threshold!

                                RUSS

Hey Jim.

                                JIM
                          (looking around)
Holy Toledo Jiminy Christmas.

                                RUSS

Bev's on the phone.

                                JIM

Hate to be the one to break it to ya, buddy, but somebody made off with yer stuff!

                                RUSS

Kinda discombobulated.

                                BEV
                            (phone)
Oh, Karl, I don't think so, not today.

                                JIM
                            (to RUSS)
S'not the big day, is it?

                         RUSS
                       (to JIM)
No no. Monday.

                         BEV
                       (phone)
No, it's just, Russ is a little under the weather.

                         JIM
Piece of advice. Watch out when you start lifting things. Learned that
the hard way last month.

                         RUSS
                 (preoccupied with BEV)
Izzat right?

                         JIM
                       (to RUSS)
Ohhhh *yeah.* Judy says Jim, I gotta have me this spinet piano, a task
which naturally falls to *me – (cont'd.)*

                         BEV
                 (phone, overlapping)
Well, if it's absolutely necessary.

                         JIM
                     (continuous)
– and there I am with this thing halfway up the front steps and me
underneath. And of course, it's not the *weight,* you know. It's the *angle –*
(cont'd.)

                         BEV
All right, Karl.

     (Hangs up.)

JIM
(continuous)
— which is why they tell ya to bend the knees.

BEV
(re: JIM)
Well, will you look what the cat dragged in?

RUSS
(to BEV, re: the phone call)
What was that about?

JIM
Bev, I am *trying* to bestow the pearls of my wisdom upon this man.

RUSS
(to JIM)
No no, I was listening.

BEV
Oh, isn't it just a *jumble* in here, all of this?

JIM
S'what I was saying to Russ, said somebody cleaned ya out!

RUSS
Not coming here, is he?

BEV
Oh, I don't know. You know Karl.

JIM
Karl Lindner?

RUSS
Bev?

JIM
Ohmigosh. Ya got a look at Betsy lately?

BEV

(eyes wide)

Oh, I *know.*

JIM

Give that girl a *wide berth.*

BEV

Jim, can I get you some iced tea?

RUSS

(to BEV)

Maybe call back and ask him to come later.

BEV

It was a pay phone.

(to JIM)

Oh oh oh oh oh! I know! Now wait. Now Jim: I am going to ask you a question:

JIM

Huh-oh!

BEV

(to RUSS).

And don't help him.

(to JIM)

Now: I want you to tell Russ what you think the word *Neapolitan* means.

RUSS

(to JIM)

She thought –

BEV

Shhhhhhh!!! You're not allowed to say.

                              JIM
Well, that'd be your basic vanilla, strawb–

                              BEV
No no. The *derivation.*

                              RUSS
I *told* her what I th–

                              BEV
                          (to RUSS)
Shhhhh!!!

                              JIM
Uh, think it's *Naples,* isn't it?

                              BEV
Ohhhhh *phooey.*

                              JIM
Or *Napoli,* as we like to say.

        (FRANCINE enters.)

                              BEV
You two are *cheating.* And then – well, Russ's in a funny mood… he
keeps going *(trying to do what RUSS did)* Oo-lan Ba-tor!

                              JIM
Whatzat, capital of Nepal?

                              RUSS
Mongolia.

                              JIM
Mongolia. So then what's the *Nepalese* – Do ya say *Nepalese?*

BEV
(chuckles, slaps RUSS's arm)
I hope it's not Ne-*politan!*

RUSS
Kathmandu.

JIM
Kathmandu!

BEV
Oh, well, I don't even know why you two know these things.

FRANCINE
Miz Stoller?

JIM
Knowledge is power, Bev.

BEV
Then I choose to remain *powerless.*

(to RUSS)
Do it again.

RUSS
Do what?

BEV
How you said it.

RUSS
No.

BEV
Do it, Russ.

RUSS
No.

BEV

Do it for Jim.

RUSS

Bev?

BEV

Why *not?*

RUSS

Sorry, Jim.

BEV

Why for me but not for him?

RUSS

Well, for one thing, 'cause it's not *funny.*

FRANCINE

Excuse me, I'm fixing to go, so if you need something else?

BEV

Oh. Yes. One thing. Francine, you remember that big trunk that's upstairs?

RUSS

No no no no. Bev?

BEV

She doesn't mind.

RUSS

Just told you I'm doing it.

BEV

You said it's a two person job, and here's two of you right here.

RUSS

Well, what's the emergency?

JIM
(to BEV)
I *would* offer my services – *(cont'd.)*

BEV
(overlapping)
Oh no no no no no.

JIM
(continuous)
but I am under doctor's orders, believe it or not.

FRANCINE
Well, I'm just needing to leave by three-thirty.

BEV
(resigned)
All right.

RUSS
Francine? *I* am going to move the gol-darned trunk.

FRANCINE
Yes, sir.

BEV
(to JIM, mock-private)
That's what I get for trying.

   (FRANCINE exits. Discomfort.)

JIM
(to RUSS)
Soooo –

BEV
Did you get any lunch, Jim? Do you want some – ?

JIM

No no no no no.

BEV

Since I guess we're *cleaning out the larder* and Russ seems to be eating every last thing in the icebox, so you'll have to fight him for the ice cream.

JIM

Not for me.

RUSS

Well, ya know. *(shrugs)* Can't pack ice cream in a suitcase.

(*BEV finds this hilarious.*)

BEV
(beside herself)

In a suitc–

(to JIM)

Did you hear what he just said?

JIM
(chuckling as well)

Man's got a point!

BEV
(slaps RUSS's shoulder)
How do you think of those things? Ice cream in a –

JIM

Not unless you're moving to the North Pole!

(*BEV laughs harder.*)

BEV

Thank goodness we're not moving *South!*

JIM

That'd be a mess. No question.

(BEV and JIM stop laughing, sigh. More discomfort, then:)

JIM

No question.

BEV
(jumping up)
Well, I'm going to see what we *do* have.

(BEV exits into the kitchen, leaving RUSS and JIM alone.)

JIM

Whaddya, coming down with something?

RUSS

Who?

JIM

Bev said "under the weather."

RUSS

Me?

JIM

And here ya sit in your PJ's –

RUSS

No no no no no. I'm – Took the day to – Truck coming, so –

JIM

I gotcha.

RUSS

Coupla days off.

JIM

Playing hooky.

RUSS

No no.

JIM

Bev's your alibi.

RUSS

Just giving her a hand with stuff.

JIM

And you are hard at work, as I see.

RUSS

(smiles a little)

No. I just.

JIM

Kidding you.

RUSS

I know. I – I – Yup.

JIM

Woulda come to your aid there, only I'm dealing with a little, uh, issue.

RUSS

Oh yeah?

JIM

Piano I told ya about?

RUSS

Right?

JIM

Didja ever... *(lowers voice)* ...ever need a *truss?* Have to wear one of those?

RUSS

Uhhhh... Don't recall.

JIM

Oh, you'd recall it if you did.

RUSS

Guess not, then.

JIM

Then you are a *fortunate* man.

RUSS

I hear you.

JIM

Bend the knees or suffer the consequences.

RUSS

Yup.

(*Brief pause.*)

JIM

So, *Monday*, you said.

RUSS

Yup.

JIM

Off to the hinterlands.

RUSS

Monday it is.

                              BEV
                        (calling from off)
Jim, was that a yes or a no on the iced tea?

                              JIM
                       (calling back to her)
Uhhh, I would not say no to that.

                              BEV
                            (same)
Russ?

        (RUSS shakes his head.)

                              JIM
                            (same)
I believe Russ is declining your gracious offer.

                              BEV
                            (same)
I thought as much.

        (Pause.)

                              JIM
Monday.

                              RUSS
Indeed.

                              JIM
Head 'em up. Move 'em out.

                              RUSS
Yup.

                              JIM
And when ya start that Glen Meadows office?

RUSS

Monday after.

JIM

How about that.

RUSS

Yup.

JIM

And how's that shaping up?

RUSS

Oh, boy, now. That's a nice setup.

JIM

I betcha.

RUSS

And *spacious*, that's the thing. And *carpeted?* And I got a look at that office they're putting me in. Tell you what I thought to myself, I thought what the heck do ya do with all this space? *Corner* office. Windows two sides. But the space is the primary – That is just an... *extravagant* amount of space.

JIM

Elbow room.

RUSS

Other thing is, once we get situated up in the new place. The time it takes? Driveway to the parking lot? Know what that's gonna take me?

JIM

Five minutes.

RUSS

Six and a half.

                              JIM

Close enough.

                              RUSS

Timed it. Door to door.

                              JIM

Roll outa bed and *boom*.

                              RUSS

And Tom Perricone. I don't know if you know Tom. Colleague of mine. Now, he's going to relocate to that same office and they live right down here offa Larabee. You know what *that's* gonna take him on the expressway?

                              JIM

That's a drive.

                              RUSS

Thirty-five minutes. And that's no traffic.

                              JIM

Well, Judy and I are sure gonna miss having you two around.

                              RUSS

Well… Yeah.

    (Awkward pause.)

                              JIM
                   (lowers voice, secretively)
And how's Bev doing?

                              RUSS

Oh, you know. Bev loves a project.

                              JIM

Keep her occupied.

The *mind* occupied.

What, does she worry a lot?

No. No more than –

About you?

Me? No.

Ya seem good to me.

I meant – you know how she gets.

Sure.

Overexcited.

I can see that.

Worked up over things. Minor things.

Things like?

Oh, you know.

JIM

Not calling yourself a *minor thing*, are you?

RUSS
(beat, slightly irritated)

No, I didn't – I meant things like –

JIM
(chuckles)

Do *you* consider yourself a *minor thing?*

RUSS

Jim, I didn't – Well, actually, in the grand scheme of things I don't think any one of us is, uh… particularly – did Bev *ask* you to come over?

JIM

Nope.

RUSS

I mean, good to see you. Great to see you.

JIM

I mean, we *ran into* each other coupla days ago. Got to talking.

RUSS

Uh-huh.

JIM

Little about you. Since she cares about you.

RUSS

Right. Right.

(RUSS looks for BEV.)

RUSS

'The heck's she's doing in there?

Everybody cares about you, Russ.

RUSS

Uh-huh. Uh-huh. Yup. Well. Tell ya what I think. And I'm not a psychiatrist or anything but I do think a lotta people today have this tendency, tendency to *brood* about stuff, which, if you ask me, is, is, is – well, short answer, it's *not productive*. And what *I'd* say to these people, *were* I to have a degree in psychiatry, I think my advice would be maybe, get up offa your rear end and *do* something.

JIM

Huh.

RUSS

Be my solution.

JIM

Uh-huh.

RUSS

Of course, what do I know?

JIM

I think you know plenty.

(Beat. RUSS looks toward kitchen.)

RUSS
(calling)

Hey, Bev?

JIM

Like, I think you know your son was a good man, no matter what. Hero to his country. Nothing changes that.

RUSS

Yup yup yup.

And I also think you know that sometimes talking about things that happen, painful things, maybe –

RUSS

Uh, you don't happen to have a degree in psychiatry *either,* do you, Jim?

(JIM stares.)

RUSS

No? Just checking.

JIM

We all suffer, you know. Not like you and Bev, maybe, but –

RUSS

But, see, since what *I'm* doing here is, see, since I'm just minding *my own* business – *(cont'd.)*

JIM
(overlapping)

But it doesn't hurt –

RUSS
(continuous)

– sorta seems to *me* you might save yourself the effort worrying about things you don't need to *concern* yourself with and furthermore – *(cont'd.)*

JIM
(overlapping)

He's in a better place, Russ.

RUSS
(cont'd.)

– if you *do* keep going on about those things, Jim, well, I hate to have to put it this way, but what I think I might have to do is… uh, politely ask you to uh, *(clears his throat)* …well, to go fuck yourself.

(Pause.)

JIM

Not sure there's a polite way to ask that.

(RUSS rises to exit.)

RUSS
(embarrassed)

Okay? So.

JIM

I just can't believe Kenneth would've wanted his own father to –

RUSS
(maintaining calm)

Yup. Yup. So, you can go fuck yourself okay?

(BEV enters with JIM's iced tea.)

BEV

So wait. So if it's *Napoli* in Italian, then wouldn't adding an "E" before the "A" just seem superfluo– What's happening?

JIM

Bev, I believe I will hit the road.

BEV

What are you – ? Russ?

RUSS

Going upstairs.

BEV

What happened?

JIM

Not to worry.

                          BEV
                       (to RUSS)
What did you do?

                          JIM
Another time.

                          BEV
                       (to RUSS)
Come back here.

                          JIM
                (overlapping, to BEV)
No no. Russ made his feelings clear in – *(cont'd.)*

                          BEV
            (overlapping, quietly to RUSS)
Why are you being like this?

                          JIM
                    (continuous)
– no uncertain terms.

                          RUSS
                       (to BEV)
Going up, now.

                          JIM
Terms maybe more appropriate for the *locker room* than the –

                          BEV
                       (to JIM)
I *told* you so. I *told* you what it's like. And he uses these ugly words in
other people's presence and I'm not some kind of *matron*, but what in
the world is wrong with *civility?*

RUSS

Honey? I am not going to stand here with you and Jim and discuss –
(cont'd.)

BEV

(overlapping)
Well, you're being *ugly*, and I don't like *ugliness*.

RUSS

(continuous)
– *private* matters, matters that are between me and the memory of my
son –

BEV

(to JIM, overlapping)
I think his *mind* has been affected, I really do.

RUSS

(continuous, overlapping)
– and if the two of you want to talk about Kenneth on your *own* time,
if that gives you some kind you *comfort* –

BEV

And what's wrong with *comfort?* Are we not *allowed* any comfort
anymore?

RUSS

Well, Kenneth didn't get a whole lotta comfort, did he?

BEV

He was *sick*, Russ! And for you to use nasty words to Jim –

JIM

Nothing I haven't heard before.

RUSS

(moving upstairs)
Changing my shirt.

JIM

I was in the service, too, you know.

RUSS
(bitter laugh)
Oh right. And tell me again. How many people did *you* kill?

BEV
Oh, for God's sake, stop it!!

RUSS
Sat behind a *desk*, didn'tcha? Goddamn *coward.*

(The doorbell rings. All stand in silence. BEV covers her mouth. At the front door, we can see ALBERT peer through a small window.)

ALBERT
(from off)
Hello?

(And still no one moves.)

ALBERT
Anybody home?

(BEV looks at JIM. JIM moves to open the door.)

JIM
Afternoon.

ALBERT
(to JIM)
Uh, how d'you do? I'm just here to –

BEV
Francine? Albert's here.

FRANCINE
(calling, from off)

Yes ma'am. I'm coming.

BEV

She's on her way.

ALBERT

Thank you, ma'am.

(JIM does not know whether to invite ALBERT in or not. He turns to BEV. RUSS turns and exits up the stairs. BEV turns back to ALBERT.)

BEV

Albert, would you like to wait inside?

ALBERT

Uh. All right, thank you, ma'am.

BEV

I bet it's warm out there, isn't it?

ALBERT

Ohhh, yes it is.

BEV

Can I offer you some iced tea?

ALBERT

No. Thank you, though.

BEV

Well, I'm sure she'll be right along.

JIM

Thank you.

(ALBERT sits near the door, but within earshot of JIM and BEV.)

JIM
(whispering because of ALBERT)
I think maybe it's time for me –

BEV
(rapidly, whispering)
Oh please don't go, please don't, I just don't want to be alone with him right now. It makes me feel so alone – *(cont'd.)*

JIM
(overlapping)
You're not alone.

BEV
(continuous)
– the way he sits up all night long. Last night he was just sitting there at three in the morning – *(cont'd.)*

JIM
(overlapping)
I know. I do.

BEV
(continuous)
– and I say to him say don't you feel sleepy? Do you want to take a Sominex, or play some cards maybe, and he says *I don't see the point of it* as if there has to be some grand justification for every single thing that a person –

(And now she notices ALBERT rising and heading for the door.)

BEV
(to ALBERT)
– Wait. Yoo-hoo?

ALBERT
(having overheard)
S'all right.

                         BEV
Something wrong?

                         ALBERT
No no.

                         BEV
She said she's on her way.

                         ALBERT
I can wait outside.

                         BEV
                    (calling off)
Francine?

                        FRANCINE
                     (from off)
I'm coming.

                         BEV
There she is.

    *(FRANCINE enters in street clothes, with a two large bags of
    hand-me-downs, She stops to put on her earrings.)*

                        FRANCINE
I'm sorry. I guess I'm moving a little slower than usual.

                         BEV
And here's Albert waiting so patiently, If only I had *door-to-door service
like Francine!*

                        FRANCINE
So, I'll see you Monday, then.

                         BEV
Albert, isn't this place just a *catastrophe?*

ALBERT

Oh, yes it is.

BEV
(to ALBERT)
I tell you, I don't know *what* I would do without a friend like Francine here, and on a *Saturday,* I mean she is just a treasure. What on earth are we going to do up there without her?

ALBERT

Well, I trust ya'll can sort things out.

BEV
(to FRANCINE)
Oh, and maybe Monday we can see about that big trunk, why don't we?

FRANCINE

We'll make sure and do that.

BEV

I'd do it myself but I'm not a big strapping man like Albert here.

JIM

Afraid I've gotta exempt myself –

BEV

Oh no no no no no. Francine and I can manage.

ALBERT

What's it, a trunk, you said?

FRANCINE
(with a shake of the head to dissuade ALBERT)
A footlocker.

ALBERT

Where's it at?

BEV

No no no no no we just need to bring it down the stairs.

ALBERT

I don't mind.

BEV

Oh, thank you, but no.

FRANCINE
(to BEV)

But definitely Monday.

ALBERT

These stairs, here?

BEV

Oh no no no – I mean, it wouldn't take but two minutes.

FRANCINE
(to BEV, re: her bags)

It's just I got these things here to take care of.

ALBERT

I can put them in the car.

JIM

Oh, got yourself a car?

ALBERT

Yes sir.

JIM
(looking out the window)

Whatzat, a Pontiac?

ALBERT

Yes, sir.

FRANCINE

(significantly, to ALBERT)

It's just that I'm afraid we're going to be late.

ALBERT

(not getting it)

Late for what?

FRANCINE

The place we gotta be?

ALBERT

The *place?*

FRANCINE

Remember?

ALBERT

(to FRANCINE)

The – What're you – ?

FRANCINE

(to BEV)

I'm sorry.

ALBERT

(to FRANCINE)

Said two minutes is all.

FRANCINE

(quiet, pointedly)

Well, I've got my *hands* full.

ALBERT

I just said I can put them in the –

FRANCINE

(testily, as they start to go)

I can put them in the car. *I* can do that.

BEV

Did you get the chafing dish?

FRANCINE

No ma'am, thank you, though.

ALBERT

(to BEV and JIM)

Be right back.

(ALBERT opens the door to reveal KARL LINDNER, about to ring the bell. He is an oddly formal and uncomfortable-seeming man.)

KARL

Ah. Unexpected. Uhhh...?

BEV

Hello, Karl.

KARL

(relieved)

Ah, Bev. Voila.

ALBERT

(to KARL, squeezing past)

Excuse us, if you don't mind?

KARL

(to ALBERT, formally)

Not at all. After *you*, sir.

(KARL makes way for ALBERT and FRANCINE to pass.)

ALBERT

(to FRANCINE, as they exit, barely audible)

What is the *matter* with you?

ACT I, 1959   47

KARL
(from the door, seeing him)
Ah. Jim, too. Hello, lad.

JIM
Karl.

BEV
(unenthusiastically)
Come on in, Karl.

KARL
(as if working out a puzzle)
Uhhh… Yes. *Could* do that. However, You'll recall, Bev, that Betsy
currently happens to be, uh, how shall we say – ?

BEV
Ohhh, is it almost that time?

KARL
Uh, point *being,* that she did accompany me.

BEV
What do you – you mean she's in the *car?*

KARL
She is.

BEV
Well, for heaven's *sake,* Karl! Don't leave her out in a hot *car.*

KARL
Well, that was my thinking.

BEV
Bring her *in* with you.

KARL
Will do.

Of all *things*.

KARL
(as he goes)

Back in a flash.

(As KARL exits again, RUSS descends the stairs in a clean shirt and shoes. BEV and JIM allow him to silently pass by them. He walks to the chair and collects the ice cream carton.)

BEV

You changed your shirt.

(RUSS continues into the kitchen without responding. As soon as he is gone:)

JIM
(quietly)

Bev.

BEV
(whispering)

I know I'm being silly. I know I am, but — *(cont'd.)*

JIM
(overlapping)

Not at all. Not in the least.

BEV
(continuous whisper)

— it's just that after two and a half *years* you'd think that with *time*, because that's supposed to be the thing that helps, isn't it? A little bit of time — *(cont'd.)*

JIM
(overlapping)

A great healer.

BEV
(continuous whisper)

– and I thought with the new job and the move I thought somehow he would start to let go of –

(RUSS returns from the kitchen. BEV goes silent. He goes to a door beneath the stairs, opens it, pulls a string to turn on a light, and exits.)

BEV
(calling after him)

Where are you going, the basement?

RUSS
(from off)

Yup.

BEV

Are you looking for something?

RUSS
(farther)

Yup.

(The front door opens. KARL escorts his wife BETSY, who is eight months pregnant, and who also happens to be totally deaf.)

KARL

Here we are, then.

BEV

Oh, *there she is!*

BETSY

Hehhyoooh, Behhhh. (tr. Hello, Bev.)

BEV
(over-enunciating for BETSY's benefit)

Well just *look* at you! My *goodness.* You are just the biggest *thing.*

BETSY

Ah nohhh! Eee toooor. Ah so beee!!! (I know! It's true. I'm so big!!!)

KARL

Took the liberty of not ringing the bell.

BEV

Betsy, you know Jim.

JIM

Indeed she does.

BETSY

Hah Jeee. (Hi Jim.)

> (JIM *shows off his sign language skills to* BETSY, *finger-spelling the last word.*)

BEV

Oh, well, now look at *that*. Look at them go. What is that about? Somebody translate!

BETSY
(laughing, to KARL)

Huhuhuuh!! *Kaaaaa!!*

JIM
(chuckling along)

Uh-oh! What did I do? Did I mis-spell?

> *(BETSY signs to KARL.)*

KARL
(chuckles)

Uh, it seems, Jim, that you, uh, told Betsy that she was expecting a *storm!!*

BEV

No! He meant stork! You meant *stork*, didn't you?

BETSY
(pantomimes umbrella)
Ahneemah-umbrayah! (I need my umbrella!)

(All laugh.)

BEV
Her *umbrella!* I understood that!

KARL
Have to check the weather report!

BEV
A *storm*, I'm going to tell that to Russ.

JIM
(conceding his mistake)
Must have rusty fingers!!

(All chuckle.)

BETSY
(to KARL, asking for translation)
Kaaaah?

KARL
(speaks as he signs)
Uh, Jim says *his fingers are rusty.*

(BETSY laughs and covers her mouth.)

BEV
See? She understands.

BETSY
(to JIM, pantomimes washing hands)
Jeee, mehbbe yew neeee sooohh!! (Jim, maybe you need soap!!)

(More polite laughing.)

BEV	JIM
(explaining to JIM)	*(to BEV)*
Soap. For the *rust* on your –	No, I understood

(RUSS emerges from the basement, carrying a large shovel.)

KARL

And there's the man himself! Thought he'd absconded!

BEV
(to RUSS)

The Lindners are here.

BETSY

Hehhyoooo, Ruuuuhhh. (Hello, Russ.)

RUSS

Betsy.

(to BEV)

Ya seen my gloves anywhere?

KARL
(re: the shovel)

Tunneling to China, are we?

RUSS
(to BEV)

Pair of work gloves?

BEV
(to KARL)

Do you know I just got through saying how Russ and I never entertain and here it is a regular neighborhood social!

KARL

Well, we shan't be long.

BEV

Karl, do you suppose Betsy would like a glass of iced tea?

KARL
(she does not see him)
Bets-?

(to BEV)
Point to me.

BEV
(to BETSY, over-enunciated)
Betsy, look at Karl.

(BETSY looks at KARL.)

KARL
(to BETSY, signing simultaneously)
Bev wants to know if you want some iced tea to drink?

BETSY

Ohhh, yehhhpeee. Dahhnyoo, Behhh. (Yes please. Thank you, Bev.)

RUSS
(to BEV)
Know the gloves I'm talking about?

BEV

Well, Karl's here. I thought you were going to talk to Karl.

(FRANCINE and ALBERT have entered and started up the stairs.)

RUSS
(seeing ALBERT and FRANCINE)
'The heck's going on?

BEV

Nothing. Now, we two girls are going to the refreshment stand, so you boys'll have to manage on your own.

KARL

Have no fear.

BEV
(while exiting, as before)
So how are you feeling, Betsy? Are you tired?

BETSY

Noooo, ahhhh fiiieee, Behhhh, reeeee. (No, I'm fine, Bev, really.)

(BETSY and BEV exit to the kitchen.)

KARL

Now, Russ, Bev tells me you're indisposed, and normally I'd – *(realizes)* Ah. Not *contagious*, is it?

RUSS

Is what?

KARL

Hate for Betsy to, uh, come into contact with any –

RUSS

Not contagious.

KARL

Can't be too careful. Or possibly one can. Anyway, hate to commandeer your Saturday afternoon here, *a man's home*, as they say, but, as we haven't seen your face at Rotary of late I thought I might – *(cont'd.)*

RUSS
(overlapping)
What's on your mind, Karl?

KARL
(continuous)

– intrude upon the sanctity of – what'd you say?

RUSS

What's on your mind?

KARL

Ah. Well. Firstly – May I sit?

RUSS

Yeah, yeah.

JIM

Karl, I will be taking my leave.

KARL

Not on my account?

JIM

Parish business.

KARL

Uh, well, truth to tell, Jim, we might actually benefit from your insight, here?

JIM
(looks at watch)

Uhhhhh –

KARL

If it's not pressing?

JIM

Actually –

KARL

Not to usurp your authority, Russ. Your castle. You are the king.

What's on your mind?

Is this safe?

Anywhere.

No breakables? And Jim?

Uhh... minute or two.

Good. Good good good. So.

> *(BEV opens the kitchen door.)*

Iced tea for you, Karl?

Ah. Problem *being* that I *do* have some sensitivity to the cold beverages, so my question would be is the tea *chilled,* by which I mean has it been *in* the Frigidaire?

No, Karl.

Then, if I might have a serving *minus* the ice? That would suit me fine.

All right, Karl.

(BEV closes the door.)

KARL

Anyway Russ, if you don't mind, I will proceed directly to, dare I say, *the crux*. So. First and foremost, as far as matters of *community* are concerned, I've always maintained –

(BEV and BETSY enter from the kitchen with glasses of iced tea.)

BEV

All right, you boys.

KARL
(panicky about BETSY)

What's – ? Is something – ?

BEV
(handing KARL his tea)

She's *fine*, Karl.

KARL

Is that tea, she's drinking?

BEV

Yes, Karl.

KARL

Slow sips. Small sips.

BEV

All right, Karl.

(BETSY and BEV sit at the dining table, away from the men. They begin to communicate via pad and pencil.)

RUSS

You were saying?

KARL
(glasses off, mops brow)

Tad overwrought, I suppose. *(lowers voice)* What with Betsy's condition, but... well, given our history of two years ago, I don't know, Russ, if you knew the details of that.

RUSS

Some, yup.

KARL

And Jim: Source of great comfort for us during all of that.

(beat, then to RUSS)

It was the umbilical cord. Nature of the problem.

RUSS

I knew that.

KARL

Wrapped around the... *(indicates his neck)* Exactly. So, no one at fault. No one to *blame*. But these tragedies do come along. As you and Bev well know.

JIM

What're you hoping? Boy or girl?

KARL

Ah, no. Touch wood. No tempting fate.

JIM

There you go.

KARL
(back to RUSS)

Not to compare *our* little... setback... to what the two of you endured, but —

RUSS

Something about a *crux?*

KARL

Right you are. Well: To backtrack. I take it, Russ, you're aware that the Community Association meets the first Tuesday of each month? And as I'm sure you know, Don Skinner is part of the steering committee. And somehow it came to Don's attention at this late juncture that Ted Driscoll had found a buyer for this house and I have to say it *did* come as something of a shock when Don told us what sort of people they were.

RUSS

What sort of people are they?

(Beat. KARL stares at RUSS.)

KARL

Well. *(chuckles)* Uhh… Huh. I suppose I'm forced to consider the possibility that you actually don't *know.*

RUSS

Don't know *what?*

KARL

Well, I mean. That they're colored.

RUSS

Who are?

KARL

The family. It's a colored family.

(Pause.)

KARL

So: I contacted the family —

JIM

Wait wait wait.

KARL

(to RUSS)

You're saying Ted never bothered to tell you?

RUSS

We, uhh… sort of gave Ted free rein on the –

JIM

I don't think you're right on this one, Karl.

KARL

Oh, but I am. Oh, I've spoken with the family.

RUSS

Bev?

JIM

On the *telephone?*

KARL

Oh, no. As a matter of fact, Betsy and I've just come directly from… *(beat, for effect)* Well, from *Hamilton Park.*

BEV

(to RUSS)

What is it?

RUSS

C'mere a second.

KARL

Now, Russ, you know as well as I do that this is a progressive community.

BEV

(to RUSS as she joins them)

What's he talking about?

KARL

If you take the case of Gelman's grocery: That's a fine example of how we've all embraced a different way of thinking –

RUSS

Slow down a second. Bev, get Ted Driscoll on the phone.

BEV

What for?

RUSS

Karl says. Karl is *claiming* –

KARL

Russ, I have met *personally* with the family, and –

BEV

What family?

RUSS

He claims this family. The family to whom Ted sold the house.

KARL

It's a colored family.

(Pause. JIM shakes his head.)

JIM

(to KARL)

Sorry, don't we say *Negro*, now?

KARL

(irritated)

I *say* Negro – *(cont'd.)*

JIM

(overlapping)

Well, it's only common courtesy, and I'm –

KARL

(continuous)

– I say them *interchangeably* – *(cont'd.)*

JIM

(overlapping)

– not trying to tell you how to conduct your business.

KARL

(continuous)

– and of course I said *Negro* to them – No I think we both know what you're doing.

JIM

And furthermore, I don't think Ted would pull a stunt like that.

KARL

Yes. We all admire Ted. But I don't think any of us would accuse him of putting the community's interests ahead of his own.

BEV

Oh, this is ridiculous.

KARL

And I don't think any of us have forgotten what happened with the family that moved onto Kostner Avenue last year. Now, Kostner Avenue is *one* thing, but *Clybourne* Street –

BEV

Waitwaitwait. Karl, are you *sure?*

KARL

I was sitting with them not two hours ago.

BEV

But isn't it possible that they're... I don't know, *Mediterranean,* or – ?

KARL

Bev, they are *one hundred percent.* And I don't know how much time any of you have spent in Hamilton Park, but Betsy was waiting in the car and I can tell you, there are some *unsavory* characters.

RUSS

Karl?

KARL

But, in the case of Gelman's: I think there was some mistrust at first, having been Kopeckne's Market for such a long time, but in the end of all Murray Gelman found a way to *fit in.*

BEV

And they hired the Wheeler boy.

JIM

Is he the one with the – ? *(taps his finger against his temple)*

BEV

He's the – you know. *(does the same)*

KARL

And *fitting into* a community is really what it all comes down to.

(A very loud THUMP from upstairs.)

RUSS

The heck is going *on* up there?

KARL

Now, some would say change is inevitable. And I can support that, if it's change for the better. But I'll tell you what I *can't* support, and that's disregarding the needs of the people who *live* in a community.

                              BEV

But don't they have needs, too?

                              KARL

Don't who?

                              BEV

The family.

                              KARL

Which family?

                              BEV

The ones who —

                              KARL

The *purchasers?*

                              BEV

I mean, in, in, in, in *principle,* don't we *all* deserve to — shouldn't we *all*
have the opportunity to, to, to —

                              KARL
              (chuckles with amazement, shakes his head)
Well, *Bev.*

                              JIM

In *principle,* no question.

                              KARL

But you can't *live* in a principle, can you? Gotta live in a *house.*

                              BEV

And so do they.

                              KARL

Not in *this* house, they don't.

JIM

But here's the real question:

KARL

And what happened to *love thy neighbor?* If we're being so principled.

BEV

They would *become* our neighbors.

KARL

And what about the neighbors you already *have* Bev?

BEV

I care about them, too!

KARL

Well, I'm afraid you can't have it both ways.

RUSS

Okay. Assuming –

BEV

Wait. Why not?

KARL

Well, do the boundaries of the neighborhood extend indefinitely?
Who shall we invite next, the *Red Chinese?*

(ALBERT has tentatively come to the bottom of the stairs, jacket off.)

JIM

But the key question is this:

BEV

No. Why *not* have it both ways?

KARL

Darling, I came to talk to Russ.

ALBERT

'Scuse me, ma'am?

BEV

Why not, if it would *benefit* someone?

JIM

But *would* they benefit?

BEV

If we could make them our *neighbors*.

KARL

But they won't be *your* neighbors, Bev. *You're* the ones moving *away!*

JIM

The question is, and it's one worth asking:

ALBERT

Sorry to bother you?

RUSS
(taking charge, ignoring ALBERT)
Okay. *(beat)* Let's *assume* your information is correct.

(Then suddenly, a large green Army footlocker comes sliding down the stairs with a noisy thumpeta-thumpeta-thumpeta-thump. ALBERT jumps out of the way.)

ALBERT	FRANCINE	BEV	RUSS
Sorry, sir, my fault! That was me. That was all my doing.	*(top of the stairs)* *That was my fault! I'm sorry!*	Oh oh oh. What happened? Is everyone all right?	Aw, for crying out loud! What the heck is the matter with people? Bev, darn it all!

BEV
(to RUSS)
Why are you shouting? Everything's *fine,* so – *(cont'd.)*

RUSS
(overlapping)
Well, what did I tell you? *(cont'd.)*

BEV
(continuous)
– please don't do that, they're just trying to *help.*

RUSS
(continuous)
I *told* you I'd do it. You heard me plain as day.

BETSY
Eeeen *ahhhh* hurrrrhhh daaaaaa! (Even *I* heard that!)

KARL
(to RUSS and BEV)
Little *mishap,* is it?

ALBERT
Little trouble making the corner, is all.

FRANCINE
(now downstairs)
I'm sorry. It's heavy and I lost my gr–

RUSS
(to ALBERT)
Just leave the darn thing where it is.

BEV	KARL	JIM	ALBERT
We can't leave it there.	May one be of asistance? –	Lend you a hand, if I could, but	What should we – ? would you prefer it if I – ?

RUSS
(to ALBERT)

Just, just, just, just *leave* it.

BEV

But it's blocking the way.

FRANCINE

No ma'am, I can step over.

ALBERT

It's all right. I got her.

(ALBERT helps FRANCINE climb over the box that now blocks the stairs.)

KARL

Anyway, let's not drag this out *ad infinitum.*

(RUSS, fed up, rises and exits to the basement, slamming the door behind him.)

BEV

Russ, *don't.*

JIM
(to KARL)

One second, if I might?

(to FRANCINE)

Sorry. Uh, *Francine,* is it?

FRANCINE

Yes sir?

JIM

Francine, we've just been having a little conversation here, and I was wondering if maybe we could spare us a couple of minutes of your time?

KARL

What good does that do? Go next door. Talk to the Olsens. Talk to those who stand to lose.

JIM
(ingoring him, to FRANCINE)
I want to pose a little hypothetical to you. What if we said this: Let's imagine you and your husband here, let's say that the two of you had the opportunity to move from your current home into a different neighborhood, and let's say that neighborhood happened to be this one.

FRANCINE

Well, I don't think that we would, financially –

JIM

But for the sake of argument. Say you had the wherewithal. Would this be the sort of neighborhood you'd find an attractive place in which to live?

(FRANCINE hesitates.)

BEV

Oh, this is so sil–

FRANCINE

It's a very nice neighborhood.

(to FRANCINE)

No, I'm asking, would the two of you – Would your fam– I assume you have children?

FRANCINE

Three children.

JIM

Oh, super. So, with your children, might this be the sort of place, bearing in mind that they, too, would stand to be affected – ?

BEV

This is confusing things! It's confusing the issue!

FRANCINE
(to JIM)

It's a *very lovely* neighborh–

JIM

No, be honest. We want you to say.

BEV
(to FRANCINE)

I think what Jim is asking, in his way –

ALBERT

He means living next to white folks.

BEV

I – I – I – I – well, yes.

(Pause.)

FRANCINE

Well –

BEV

Francine and I have, over the years, the *two of us* have shared so many wonderful –

(to FRANCINE)

– Remember that time the *squirrel* came through the window?

FRANCINE
(smiling, indulging BEV)

Yes, I do.

BEV

That was just the silliest – the two of us were just *hysterical* weren't we?

KARL
(pressing ahead, to FRANCINE)

Think of it this way.

BEV
(to the others)

We still laugh about that.

KARL

I think that you'd agree, I'm assuming, that in the world, there exist certain *differences*. Agreed?

FRANCINE

What sort of differences?

KARL

That people *live* differently.

FRANCINE
(unsure)

...Yes?

KARL

From one another.

FRANCINE

I agree with that.

KARL

Different customs, different… well, different *foods,* even. And those
diff– here's a funny – my wife Betsy, now, Betsy's family happens to
be Scandinavian, and on holidays they eat a thing known as *lutefisk*.
And this is a dish, which I can tell you… *(he chuckles)* …is *not* to my
liking *at all.* It's… *oh* my goodness, let's just say it's *gelatinous.*

BEV
(indicating for him to stop)

Karl?

BETSY
(to BEV)

Whaaaaa sehhhhh? (What did he say?)

BEV
(over-pronouncing for BETSY)

Lutefisk.

BETSY

Whaaaaaa?

BEV

Lutefi– Karl, can you tell her?

KARL
(holds up a finger to BETSY)

In a moment.

BEV
(taking up her pad)

I'll write it down.

KARL
(to FRANCINE)
So, certain groups, they tend to *eat* certain things, am I right?

FRANCINE
I've never had that dish.

KARL
But, for example, if Mrs. Stoller here were to send you to shop
at Gelman's. Do you find, when you're standing in the aisles *at*
Gelman's, does it generally strike you as the kind of market where
you could find the particular foods *your* family enjoys?

FRANCINE
It's a *very* nice store.

JIM
(interposing)
What if we were to say *this:*

FRANCINE
Mr. Gelman's a nice man.

(BEV hands BETSY the pad of paper.)

KARL
But, I mean, your *preferred* food items, would such things even be
available at Gelman's?

ALBERT
Do they *carry* collards and pig feet?

(FRANCINE shoots a look at ALBERT.)

ALBERT
'Cuz I sho couldn't shop nowhere didn' sell no pig feet.

(Pause. All stare at ALBERT.)

JIM

Well, I think Albert's being *humorous* here, but —

BETSY
(having deciphered BEV's handwriting)

Ohhhh, *loo-feee!* (Lutefisk!)

(to BEV)

Ah *lye* loofee! (I *like* Lutefisk!)

JIM

But I will say this —

FRANCINE
(to KARL)

I like spaghetti and meatballs.

(KARL quiets BETSY.)

JIM

— You do find differences in modes of *worship*. If you take First
Presbyterian. Now, that's a church down in Hamilton Park and I've
taken fellowship there and I can tell you, the differences are notable.

BEV

Jim?

JIM

Not a *value* judgment. Apples and oranges. Just as how we have our
organ here at Saint Thomas, for accompaniment, whereas at First
Presbyterian, they prefer a piano and, occasionally… *(chuckles)*…well,
tambourines.

BEV

What's wrong with tambourines?

JIM

Nothing *wrong.*

I *like* tambourines.

I like tambourines as much as the next person.

(RUSS returns from the basement. He is calmer.)

Well, let me ask this.

(to BEV)

Excuse me.

(to FRANCINE)

Francine, was it?

Yessir.

Francine, may I ask? Do you *ski?*

Do I – ?

Or your husband? Either of you?

Ski?

Downhill skiing?

We don't ski, no.

KARL

And this is my point. The children who attend St. Stanislaus. Once a year we take the middle schoolers up to Indianhead Mountain, and I can tell you, in all the time I've been there, I have not *once* seen a colored family on those slopes. Now, what accounts for that? Certainly not any deficit in ability, so what I have to conclude is that, for some reason, there is just something about the pastime of skiing that doesn't appeal to the Negro community. And feel free to prove me wrong.

RUSS

Karl.

KARL

But you'll have to show me where to find the skiing Negroes!

RUSS

Karl!

BEV

Can we all modulate our voices?

RUSS

It's sold, Karl. The house is sold.

KARL

I understand that.

RUSS

The ink is dry.

KARL

And we all understand your reasons and no one holds that against you.

RUSS

Truck's coming on Monday.

KARL

Fully aware.

                              RUSS
And that's all there is to that.

                              KARL
However. There is *one* possibility.

                              RUSS
Nope. Nope.

                              KARL
If you'll hear me out.

                              RUSS
Don't see the point.

                              KARL
Because we went ahead and made a counter-offer to these people.

                              BEV
Who did?

                              KARL
The Community Association.

                              BEV
An offer on *this* house?

                              KARL
Very reasonable offer.

                              BEV
                           (baffled)
But, but, but, they just *bought* it, Karl!

                              KARL
As opposed to the amount for which *you* offered the property, Russ,
which was *far* below the assessor's value – *(cont'd.)*

RUSS
(overlapping)
Well, we're entitled to *give* it away if that's our prerogative.

KARL
(continuous)
– for this type of residence, all of which is neither here nor there,
since the family *rejected* our offer. However:

RFV
(to RUSS)
Why are we even *talking* about this?

KARL
Don *has* pointed out to me, that, as the seller of the property, you do
have a sixty-day option to place it in receivership with the transacting
bank to indemnify yourself against liability. Now, that's generally with
commercial properties, but in this instance – *(cont'd.)*

RUSS
(slowly, overlapping)
Nope. Nope. Nope. Nope. Nope.

KARL
(continuous)
– I think that, inasmuch as Ted *deceived* you about the buyers, that the
bank *could* still halt the sale and it would be a simple – *(cont'd.)*

RUSS
(overlapping)
Karl?

KARL
(continuous)
– matter of a signature, if I could finish?

RUSS
Prefer it if you didn't.

Kaahhhh?

BEV

And for all we know this family could be perfectly lovely.

KARL

Well, that's hardly the point, is it?

BEV

Maybe it's a point to consider.

KARL
(with a chuckle)
Bev, I'm not here to solve society's problems. I'm simply telling you what will happen, and it will happen as follows: First one family will leave, then another, and another, and each time they do, the values of these properties will decline, and once that process begins, once you break that egg, Bev, all the kings horses, etcetera – *(cont'd.)*

BETSY
(overlapping)
Kaahhh?

KARL
(continuous)
– and *some* of us, you see, those who *don't* have the opportunity to simply pick up and move at the drop of a hat, then *those* folks are left holding the bag, and it's a fairly *worthless* bag, at that point.

BEV

I don't like the tone this is taking.

RUSS
(to KARL)
Okay. Tell you what.

KARL

And let's imagine if the tables were turned. *(re: FRANCINE and ALBERT)* Suppose a number of *white* families started marching into *their* commun– ? Well, actually that might be to their *advantage*, but –

RUSS

Karl.

KARL

– you do see my point.

RUSS

Need you to stop now.

KARL

Sorry. *(beat)* Maybe not handled with the –

RUSS

It's all right.

KARL

– utmost delicacy.

RUSS

But maybe time to let it drop.

KARL

Didn't mean to turn it into a public referendum. *(beat)* But you do understand –

RUSS

No no no no no. That's it. You hear me? Done. All done.

(Pause. In the near distance a church bell begins to ring.)

JIM
(quietly, looking at his watch)

Is it four o'clock?

                              KARL

Well, Russ, if I might –

                              RUSS

Nope. Nope.

                              KARL

If I could just say this:

                              RUSS

No. Karl?

                              KARL

Well, if you'd let me –

                              RUSS

No. No more.

                              KARL

Uhhh… *(chuckling) Bev?* I get the impression your husband is telling
me I'm not permitted to *speak*.

                              RUSS

Don't think it's a good idea.

                              KARL

Well, Russ, I'm going to ask you at least to keep an open – ?

                              RUSS

Karl! What'd I just ask you?

                              KARL

Well, I think you're being a tad unreasonable.

                              RUSS

Well, *I* think we've reached the end of this particular discussion.

                              KARL

Is that right?

RUSS

Afraid it is.

KARL

Just like that.

RUSS

Just like that.

(Another pause.)

KARL

Then what about this:

RUSS

Karl!?

KARL

Well, I believe the Constitution endows me with a *right* to speak.

RUSS

Well, then you can go and do that in your own home.

(RUSS crosses and opens the front door for KARL to exit.)

KARL

Bev…? *(laughs)* He's not being serious, is he?

RUSS

Karl?

KARL
(laughs)

Am I being *silenced?*

RUSS

Not going to ask you again.

KARL

Well, this is a new experience for me.

RUSS

So be it.

KARL

Bit like the Soviet Union. *(laughs)* I am truly surprised.

RUSS

Well, *surprise.*

KARL

And a little disappointed.

RUSS

Sorry to disappoint you.

KARL
(shakes his head)
A real shame. For all concerned.

RUSS

Well, that's the way things go sometimes.

KARL

Apparently so.

RUSS

Anyway. Appreciate you stopping by.

KARL

I see.

RUSS

Betsy, too.

KARL

Very well.

BETSY

Kaaaaahhhh?

RUSS

Okay then? Okay.

(Silence. KARL stands and looks to BETSY. The two of them slowly exit through the open door, RUSS quietly closing it as they go.)

BETSY
(quietly, before the door is closed)

Kaahhh, whaah happaaahh?

FRANCINE
(carefully)

Miz Stoller, if we're done talking here?

JIM
(rising)

Yes, you know, I think *I* will take this opportunity –

(But KARL abruptly returns, BETSY following.)

KARL

However:

JIM
(quietly)

Karl, don't.

KARL
(very slowly)

I *don't* imagine that... this particular family are *entirely* aware of *why* they've found such an agreeable price for the property. Don't suppose they know *that* aspect of it, do they? And let's say someone was to *inform* them of those facts. Let's say *that* was to happen.

RUSS
(chuckles dangerously)
Really don't know when to quit, do ya?

KARL

Because I think that might be an interesting conversation to have.

FRANCINE
(to BEV)
So I'll be seeing you on Mon–

RUSS
(maintaining control)
Well, Karl? You go ahead and do what you think is right, but I'll tell
you one thing. What you're going to do right *now* is – *(cont'd.)*

KARL
(overlapping)
Well, I have a responsibility to the community as a whole. I can't
afford to – *(cont'd.)*

RUSS
(continuous)
– you're going to take yourself right through that door and out of
this house.

KARL
(overlapping, continuous)
– simply pursue my own selfish interests.

RUSS
(maintaining calm)
Man, what a son of a bitch.

BEV

Russ, *don't.*

RUSS

(to KARL)

If you honestly think I give a rat's ass about the goddamn – *(cont'd.)*

JIM

(overlapping)

Okay. Okay.

RUSS

(continuous)

– what, ya mean the *community* where every time I go for a haircut, where they all sit and stare like the goddamn grim reaper walked in the barber shop door? *That* community? *(cont'd.)*

KARL

(overlapping)

My wife is two weeks away from giving birth to a *child*.

RUSS

(continuous)

Where, Bev stops at Gelman's for a quart of milk and they look at her like she's got the goddamn plague? That the community I'm supposed to be looking out for?

KARL

A community with soon-to-be *children*.

JIM

The Apostle Matthew –

RUSS

(to JIM)

Oh no no no. *I'm* talking now.

BEV

(to FRANCINE and ALBERT)

I am ashamed of every one of us.

BETSY
(tugging at KARL's sleeve)

Kaaaaaah?

KARL

Betsy, wait in the car.

RUSS

Well, you go right ahead and you tell those folks whatever you want, Karl. And while you're at it why don't you tell 'em about everything *the community* did for my son. I mean Jesus Christ, Murray Gelman even goes and hires a goddamn *retarded* kid, but *my* boy? Sorry. No work for *you*, bub.

JIM

People were frightened, Russ.

RUSS
(contemptuous)

Ahh, of *what?* He was gonna *snap?* Gonna go and kill another bunch of people? Send him off to defend the goddamn country, he does like he's *told* only to find out the kinda sons-of-bitches he's defending?

BEV
(forthright)

He did not do the things they claimed he did. He would never –

RUSS

Ah, Jesus, of course he did, Bev! He confessed to what he did! Sit around all day with your head in the sand, it doesn't change the facts of what he *did*.

BEV

Not to innocent people in that country. And not to women or children. I mean, maybe he lost his temper in a –

RUSS

Ah, for Christ's sake. What do you think happens in a goddamn war? They told him to *secure the territory,* not go knocking on doors asking *permission.* And if he was man enough to admit what he did, maybe you oughta have the decency to do the same damn thing.

BEV
(turning to FRANCINE for support)
You remember. Francine remembers what he was like.

(RUSS makes a sound of disgust and goes to the footlocker. Under the following, he unlocks and opens the lid.)

BEV
How he loved to read and think. That's just the kind of boy he was, wasn't it?

FRANCINE
Yes ma'am.

BEV
(to FRANCINE)
And the drawings? The most realistic drawings. I think a lot of people didn't realize –

KARL
Bev, it was never my intention to stir up – *(cont'd.)*

BEV
Ohhh, no, I think maybe it was.

KARL
(continuous)
– such acrimonious feelings, but there is a situation, which –

BEV
Well, maybe if you had known my son a little better. If anyone had taken the time, the way that Francine took the time –

(RUSS has produced an envelope from the footlocker. He steps forward removing the letter – on yellow legal paper.)

Here you go, Karl. Let's all read a little something, shall we?

BEV

What are you – ?

RUSS
(reading)

Dear Mom and Dad.

BEV
(realizing)

Stop it!!!

RUSS
(reading)
I know you'll probably blame yourselves –

BEV
(losing it completely)
Russ, stop it stop it stop stop stop it!!!!

JIM   KARL
Russ. Don't.   *(to RUSS)*
                                             I think you're unstable, Russ. I
                                             really do.

BEV
(turning back to JIM)
You see what this is like? You see?

(to RUSS)
Well, I refuse to live this way any longer!!

(She goes into the bathroom and slams the door behind her.)

RUSS
(starting over, calmly)

Dear Mom and Dad.

JIM

Russ?

RUSS

I know you'll probably blame yourselves for what I've done —

JIM

Need you to calm down.

RUSS

And *you* can go fuck yourself.

KARL

Well, *that* is over the line, mister. That is not language I will tolerate in front of my wife.

RUSS
(beat, then:)

She's *deaf,* Karl!! Completely — *(waving to BETSY, fake-jolly)* Hello, Betsy! Go fuck yourself!

(BETSY smiles, waves back.)

RUSS

So here's what I'll do for you, Karl: Make ya ten copies of this you can hand 'em out at Rotary. Or better yet. Put it in the newsletter. Rotary news: Kid comes back from Korea, goes upstairs and wraps an extension cord around his neck. Talk *that* over at the lunch buffet next week.

BETSY
(barely audible)

Kaahhh?

RUSS

And Francine walking in at nine in the morning to find him there.
You be my guest, Karl. You go ahead and tell those people what kind
of house they're moving into and see if *that* stops 'em, because I'll
tell you what, I don't care if a hundred Ubangi tribesman with a bone
through the nose overrun this goddamn place, 'cause I'm *through with
all of you*, ya motherfucking sons of bitches. *Every one* of you.

  *(All stand in silence. We can hear BEV crying from behind the
  bathroom door. RUSS slowly folds the letter. Finally:)*

JIM

Maybe we should bow our heads for a second.

RUSS
(advancing on him)
Well, maybe I should punch you in the face.

  *(RUSS moves toward JIM, who, in backing away, inadvertently
  tumbles backwards over a box, toppling a floor lamp as he goes.)*

ALBERT	KARL	BETSY	FRANCINE
Whoa whoa whoa whoa *whoa!!*	Easy now. Easy does it… careful – Betsy, go! Betsy?	Kaahh!! Waaahhhh happneee!?	What in god's name is *wrong* with alla you people?
			(to ALBERT) Stay out of out of it. Don't. Just stay out –

 *(BETSY runs out the front door. ALBERT puts his hand on RUSS's
 shoulder.)*

ALBERT

Hang on. Let's be civilized, now.

RUSS

(whirling on ALBERT)

Ohoho, don't you touch *me*.

ALBERT

Whoa whoa whoa.

RUSS

Putting your hands on *me?* No *sir*. Not in *my* house you don't.

JIM

(gritting his teeth as he copes with his hernia)

I'm all right.

FRANCINE

(to ALBERT)

What the hell d'you think *you're* doing?

ALBERT

Who're you talking to?

FRANCINE

Who do you *think?*

KARL

(to RUSS, as he helps JIM to his feet.)

Very manly, Russ Threatening a *minister*.

ALBERT

(to FRANCINE)

Why're you talking to me like th– ?

KARL

(to RUSS)

Very *masculine*.

(KARL and JIM exit out the front door.)

FRANCINE
(to ALBERT)
I think they're *all* a buncha idiots. And who's the biggest idiot of all
to let yourself get dragged into the middle of it? Whatcha gonna be
now, the big *peacemaker* come to save the day?

(KARL sticks his head back in.)

KARL
(through the open door)
You're mentally unstable, Russ!

FRANCINE
(to ALBERT)
Let 'em knock each other's *brains* out, for all *I* care. I'm done working
for these people two days from now, and you never worked for 'em at
all, so what the hell do you care *what* they do? And now I am going to
the goddamn *car.*

*(FRANCINE exits. During the marital squabble, RUSS has
returned the letter to the footlocker and dragged it out through the
kitchen. ALBERT is now left alone in the middle of the room. He
stands idly for a moment, then moves to right the overturned floor
lamp. As he does, BEV enters from the bathroom, blowing her nose.)*

ALBERT
(seeing BEV)
It's all right. Nothing broken.

BEV
(as composed as possible)
Oh oh oh don't mind that. But thank you so much.

ALBERT
No trouble.

BEV

And do let me offer you some money for your help.

ALBERT

Oh no ma'am, that's all right.

BEV

Ohhh, are you sure?

ALBERT

Yes, ma'am.

BEV
(finding her purse)
Well, here, then. Let me at least give you fifty cents.

ALBERT

No, now you keep your money.

BEV

Or, how about dollar? Take a dollar. I don't care.

ALBERT

Ma'am?

BEV

Or take two. It's just money.

ALBERT

Happy to help.

BEV

Or take something. You have to take something.

ALBERT

No ma'am. But –

BEV

What about this chafing dish? Did you see this dish?

ALBERT

Well, we got plenty of dish–

BEV

Not one of these. Francine told me. *(cont'd.)*

ALBERT

Well, that's very kind of you, but –

BEV

She said you didn't have one and somebody should take it and –
(cont'd.)

ALBERT
(overlapping)

But we don't *need* it, ma'am.

BEV
(continuous)

– make use of it, so if you let me just wrap it for you.

ALBERT
(finally raising his voice)

Ma'am, we don't *want* your things. *Please*. We got our *own* things.

(Pause. BEV is shocked.)

BEV

Well.

ALBERT
(gently)

Trying to *explain* to you.

BEV

Well, if *that's* the attitude, then I just don't know what to say anymore.
I really don't. If that's what we're coming to.

ALBERT

Ma'am, everybody's sorry for your loss.

BEV

(holding back tears, nobly righteous)
You know, I would be... So *proud*. So *honored* to have you and
Francine as our neighbors. *And* the two children.

ALBERT

Three children.

BEV

Three chil— We would... Maybe we should *learn* what the other
person eats. Maybe that would be the solution to some of the – If
someday we could all sit down together, at one big table and, and,
and, and... *(trails into a whisper, shakes her head.)*

ALBERT

Evening, ma'am.

*(ALBERT goes. BEV is left alone. After a moment, RUSS enters
to fetch the shovel. He carries a pair of work gloves. Seeing BEV, he
stops, unsure of what to say.)*

BEV

Where'd you find the gloves?

RUSS

Under the sink.

BEV

And where are you going to dig the hole?

RUSS

Under the, uh... What's that big tree called?

BEV

The crepe myrtle.

RUSS

Under that.

BEV

Kind of late now, isn't it?

RUSS
(shrugs)

Do it tomorrow.

(*He leans the shovel against the wall. Pause. He stands idly, apologetically.*)

RUSS

Kinda lost my temper.

BEV
(nods, then)

Well, that's what happens. As we know.

(*He slowly moves to sit in the chair he sat in at the start of the act, then looks back at BEV.*)

RUSS

Know what I did the other day? Up there at the house?

BEV

What?

RUSS

Driveway to the office. Timed it. Know how long that's gonna take me now?

BEV

Five minutes?

RUSS

Six and a half.

                              BEV
Well, you'll have a leisurely breakfast.

                              RUSS
Read the paper. Cup of coffee and *bang*.

                              BEV
Hmm.

                              RUSS
Five-oh-seven, right back at your doorstep.

                              BEV
And what'll I do in between?

        (RUSS *is caught off-guard.*)

                              RUSS
I, I, uhhh... Well, gee, I guess, whatever you... Any number of...

                              BEV
Things.

                              RUSS
Projects.

                              BEV
Projects.

                              RUSS
To keep ya occupied.

                              BEV
I suppose you're right.

        (He turns on the radio. Music. He looks back at BEV, who stares
        into space.)

RUSS
(feebly, with a little sweep of the arm)

Ulan Bator!

(BEV smiles vaguely. The lights slowly fade. End of Act I.)

Act II

(September 2009. Three o'clock, Saturday afternoon. There is an overall shabbiness to the place that was not the case fifty years earlier. The wooden staircase railing has been replaced with a cheaper metal one. The oak mantelpiece and most of the woodwork have been painted over several times, the fireplace opening is bricked in, linoleum covers large areas of the wooden floor and plaster has crumbled from the lath in places. The kitchen door is now missing, and we can see through to an exterior door. The front door stands propped open.)

(Lights rise to find six people facing each other in a rough circle. To one side, STEVE and LINDSEY with KATHY, and to the other KEVIN and LENA with TOM, all dressed in generic casual clothes for a weekend afternoon. It is warm, and some have iced drinks. LINDSEY is visibly pregnant. They sit upon improvised seating – crates, abandoned furniture, etc. STEVE, LINDSEY and KATHY study xeroxed documents while the others watch. Finally:)

TOM

Everybody good?

LINDSEY

I'm good.

STEVE

Good by me.

KATHY

Go for it.

TOM

So, I guess we should start right at the top.

STEVE

Question?

                              TOM
And I know we all got questions.

                              STEVE
The terminology?

                              TOM
So let's go one at a time: Steve.

                              STEVE
The term *frontage?*

                              TOM
Right.

                              STEVE
Frontage means?

                              LINDSEY
Where are we looking?

                              STEVE
First page.

                              TOM
Frontage means –

                    (deferring to KATHY)
Did you want to – ?

                              KATHY
                         (to STEVE)
Means the portion facing the street.

                              TOM
Thus, *front.*

                              STEVE
                         (to TOM)
Portion of the *property?*

KATHY
(to STEVE)

Of the structure.

STEVE
(to TOM)

Or portion of the *structure?*

TOM

The *façade*

LINDSEY

I'm not seeing it.

KATHY

Second paragraph.

TOM

Bottom of the page.

STEVE

Where it says "minimum recess of frontage"?

TOM

Meaning, distance *from*.

KATHY
(to STEVE)

From the edge of the *property*.

TOM

Exactly.

STEVE

Is what?

TOM

Is the "recess".

                          STEVE
Not the *frontage*.

                          TOM
The frontage is what you're measuring *to*.

                          LINDSEY
Got it.

                          STEVE
I'm confused.

                          LINDSEY
And "edge of the property" means as measured from the *curb?*

                          KATHY
Correct.

                          TOM
Not from the *sidewalk?*

                          KATHY
From the curb.

                          TOM
Uhh – I'll check, but I don't think that's right.

                          KATHY
Up to and including.

                          TOM
But the sidewalk falls under the easement.

                          KATHY
Right?

                          TOM
So if it's part of the easement then it can't be part of the property, *per se*.

KATHY
(shaking her head)
By definition the property is inclusive of the easement. The easement
is legal passage *across* the property.

TOM
I don't think you're right.

KATHY
So, my understanding has always been —

KEVIN
Sorry, but — Does any of that really *matter?*

STEVE
It might.

KEVIN
I mean, I don't see how any of that really — *(cont'd.)*

STEVE
(overlapping)
The language?

KEVIN
(continuous)
— impacts the outcome of the specific problem that —

STEVE
But *I* don't want to get in a situation where we *thought* we found
a solution only to have it turn out we're screwed because of the
language.

TOM
Wait.

LINDSEY
(to STEVE)
The language is clear to *me.*

TOM
(easily)

And who's being *screwed?*

STEVE

No no no.

TOM

No one's *screwing* any—

STEVE

I didn't mean like *screwed over,* I meant like maybe we *screwed ourselves.*

KEVIN

But how does that address the *height* issue?

TOM

The elevation.

STEVE
(to TOM)

But if the elevation is *conditional* on the perimeter, right?

TOM

That's the idea.

STEVE

If I'm reading correctly?

LINDSEY

But the perimeter isn't changing.

STEVE

But we're saying if it *could.*

LINDSEY

But we've established that it can't.

STEVE

But let's say it *did.*

LINDSEY

But I'm saying it won't.

STEVE

But I'm saying *what if?*

LINDSEY

But I'm saying *what did we discuss?*

    (KATHY's cell phone rings.)

STEVE
(to LINDSEY, with an easy laugh)
Okay, but do you have to *say* it like that?

LINDSEY

Like what?

STEVE

In that *way?*

LINDSEY

What *way?*

KATHY
(looking at her phone)
It's Hector. I'd better –

STEVE
(aploqizing to KEVIN & LENA for LINDSEY)
Sorry.

LINDSEY
(to KEVIN & LENA)
Did I say something in a *way?*

LENA

Not that I noticed.

KATHY
(answering phone)

Hi, Hector.

STEVE
(explaining to KEVIN & LENA)

The architect.

LINDSEY

Who really oughta be here.

KATHY
(phone)

No, we're doing it now. No, we're here at the house.

KEVIN
(to LINDSEY)

Well, if you'd rather wait and do this when he *can* be?

STEVE

No no no.

LINDSEY
(to STEVE)

Well, I think we both know what's going to happen. *(cont'd.)*

LINDSEY *(continuous)* He's going to go completely ballist– I'm just telling you what to expect.	STEVE I don't give a – And, I believe he's working for *us*, right? Not the other way around.

KATHY
(phone)

No, we're here with –

(to TOM)

Tom, I forgot your last name.

TOM

Driscoll.

KATHY
(back to phone)
Driscoll. So, Tom Driscoll and the people from the neighborhood
thing. Property-owners... thing.

LINDSEY
(to STEVE & LENA)
And can I just say? I am in *love* with this neighborhood.

KEVIN

Great neighborhood.

LINDSEY

Totally great.

KATHY
(into phone)
Well, that's what we're trying to prevent.

LINDSEY

And the thing for me is? My current commute? Which is slowly
eroding my soul?

KEVIN
(to LINDSEY)
How far ya coming from?

LINDSEY
(pointedly)

Glen Meadows?

KEVIN
(wincing)

Ooof.

LINDSEY

Exactly. And if you work downtown?

KEVIN

Where downtown?

LINDSEY
(do you know it?)

Donnelly & Faber?

KEVIN

On Jackson, right? Donnelly & – ?

LINDSEY

Yeah, Jackson east of –

KEVIN

Yeah, I'm across the street.

LINDSEY

Where?

KEVIN

You know the big red building?

LINDSEY

I eat lunch in that building.

KEVIN

Capital Equities?

STEVE

You're kidding me.

KEVIN

I kid you not.

LINDSEY
(to KEVIN)

And from *here* to downtown is like, what, five minutes?

STEVE
(to KEVIN)

Ya ever meet Kyle Hendrickson?

KEVIN

I *work* with Kyle Hendrickson.

KATHY
(phone)

No, but I do think you're being a *little* paranoid, because we're not going to let that happen.

LINDSEY
(to KATHY)

Lemme talk to him.

KATHY

I'm not going to let it happen.

LINDSEY

Kathy.

KATHY

Wait. Lindsey wants to —

LINDSEY

Lemme do it. *(taking phone)* Hector?

KATHY
(rolling her eyes)

I'm obviously not equipped to deal with —

LINDSEY
(on phone)

I thought you were in Seattle.

STEVE
(to KATHY)

What's the problem?

KATHY

Tell you later.

LINDSEY
(soothing)

No no no no. Kathy's here. Kathy's not going to let that —

STEVE
(to the others)

Spaniards.

LINDSEY
(whispering to the others)

Two seconds.

(LINDSEY exits out the front door. Pause. The others wait.)

KEVIN
(to STEVE)

Spaniards?

STEVE

Architect, ya know.

KEVIN

Spanish.

STEVE

Temperamental.

KEVIN

Toro toro.

STEVE

Exactly.

TOM

Seemed cool to me.

                              STEVE
You talked to him?

                               TOM
On the phone, yeah.

                              STEVE
He's a good guy.

        (Little pause. Then, small talk.)

                              KATHY
We were in Spain last year.

                              KEVIN
S'that right?

                              KATHY
Me, my husband. Spain, Morocco.

                              STEVE
                    (explaining to KEVIN)
I just meant – with all the paperwork and everything? And then we
add *him* into the mix?

                              KEVIN
I hear you.

                              STEVE
Cooler heads, ya know.

                              KEVIN
Prevail.

                              STEVE
Right.

        (Little pause. Then, more small talk.)

KATHY

Spain's fantastic. We did four days in Barcelona. Saw the what's-it-called? The cathedral? Big, crazy – ?

TOM

Sagrada Familia.

KATHY

That. Which I loved. Likewise the food. Which I would happily eat every day for the rest of my life.

KEVIN

Paella.

KATHY

Then Morrocco. To whatsit. To Marrakech. Which – I don't know how you feel about *heat?* But oh my god. And they keep giving you *hot tea.* Like, how refreshing. And some theory about how you're supposed to *sweat* in order to feel *cool,* which you'll have to explain to me sometime.

TOM
(to himself)

Hot in *here.*

LENA

Very hot.

KATHY

And. To top it off. I don't want to bore you with the whole ugly saga *but:* When they tell you not to eat the produce? Take heed.

KEVIN

Like Mexico.

KATHY

Because if you ever need to know where to find a doctor at two in the morning in the capital of Morocco when your husband is doubled over with *dysentery* – ?

KEVIN

Whoa.

KATHY

Gimme a call.

(All look at door for LINDSEY's return.)

TOM
(re: LINDSEY's absence)

Said two seconds.

KEVIN
(to KATHY, indicating himself and LENA)

Went to *Prague* last April.

KATHY
(to LENA)

Oh, I *love* Prague. Prague is beautiful.

KEVIN

Very pretty.

KATHY

The architecture?

KEVIN

That bridge?

KATHY

And it's small, is what's nice. So you can do it all in a couple of days.

KEVIN

And then from there to Zurich.

KATHY

Never been to Switzerland. *(with a laugh)* But I like the cheese!

LENA

(formally)

Can I – ? I'm sorry. I didn't mean to – but I was hoping I could say something to everyone, if you don't mind?

(All pause for LENA.)

LENA

As long as we're stopped?

KATHY	KEVIN	TOM
No. Do. By all means.	Go ahead.	Yeah yeah, please.

LENA

All right, well… *(clears her throat)* Um, I just feel like it's very important for me to express, before we start getting into the details–

STEVE

Sorry, but – Maybe we should wait for Lindsey? Don't you think? If it's something important? Otherwise –

KEVIN

(to LENA)

Do you mind?

STEVE

Wind up repeating yourself.

TOM

(to LENA)

That okay with you?

LENA

It's fine with me.

                              STEVE
But, hold that thought.

                              LENA
I will.

    (*Little pause.* TOM *drums his fingers.*)

                              STEVE
Meanwhile –

                              TOM
Meanwhile maybe we should look at page three?

                              KATHY
Maybe we should.

                              TOM
Catch her up when she –

                    (to STEVE)
– if that's cool with you guys.

                              STEVE
S'cool with me.

                              TOM
Good.

                              KEVIN
Let's do it.

                              TOM
Just 'cuz I gotta be outa here by like four.

                              STEVE
Forge ahead.

KATHY

Page three.

TOM

Middle of three.

KATHY

Section two.

TOM

Roman numeral two.

STEVE

(aside to KATHY, quietly)

Rabat, by the way.

TOM

Whadja say?

STEVE

Nothing.

KATHY

Couldn't hear you.

STEVE

The capital.

TOM

Of what?

STEVE

Morocco. She said Marrakech.

KATHY

It *is* the capital.

STEVE

No.

                              TOM
I'd've said Marrakech.

                              STEVE
Rabat

                              KATHY
I don't think you're right.

                              STEVE
No, it is.

                              KATHY
But possibly.

                              STEVE
Definitely. Anyway.

                              TOM
Anyway –

                              KATHY
Or, wait. Is it *Tangiers?*

                              STEVE
Nope.

                              KATHY
Why am I thinking Tangiers?

                              STEVE
Dunno.

                              KATHY
Maybe we just *landed* in Tang– Or wait, no we didn't.

                              KEVIN
                          (to STEVE)
What's the capital?

                          KATHY

I know what it is. Tangiers was the *old* capital.

                          STEVE

Umm... no?

                          KATHY

The *historic* capital.

          (LINDSEY returns.)

                          LINDSEY

So sorry.

                          KEVIN

Everything all right?

                          LINDSEY
          (returning KATHY's phone)
It's fine. It's just, he said he was going to be in Seattle so we went
ahead and scheduled this without him and now he's feeling a little
proprietary – Anyway. Blah blah.

                          TOM

So, we skipped ahead.

                          LINDSEY

Great.

                          TOM

To page three?

                          KATHY

Middle of three.

                          TOM

And since I think we'd all basically agree that –

                              STEVE
                          (to LINDSEY)
Hey.

                              (to TOM)
Sorry.

                          (to LINDSEY)
What's the capital of Morocco?

                              LINDSEY
The what?

                              STEVE
The capital.

                              LINDSEY
What are you talking about?

                              STEVE
Of Morocco.

                              LINDSEY
Why?

                              STEVE
Quick. Just –

                              LINDSEY
I have no idea.

                              STEVE
Yes you do.

                              KATHY
I said Marrakech.

STEVE	LINDSEY
(to KATHY)	Marrakech, yeah.
No no, Let her –	

STEVE

No. *Rabat.*

LINDSEY

Whatever.

KEVIN
(explaining to LINDSEY)

Trying to figure out what it was.

LINDSEY

Why?

STEVE

She said she went to the capital of Morocco –

LINDSEY

So?

STEVE

– and it's not the capital.

LINDSEY
(with a shrug)

Maybe they changed it.

STEVE
(beat, then)

Who?

LINDSEY

The Moroccans.

                          STEVE
To what?

                          LINDSEY
Whatever it is now.

                          STEVE
Which is *Rabat*.

                          LINDSEY
Okay.

                          TOM
So –

                          KATHY
Oh, wait. You know what it is? It's *Timbuktu*.

                          STEVE
...*nnnnnnno?*

                          KATHY
The old capital. The historic – *(tapping her temple)* That's why I –
because it was part of our package.

                          STEVE
Um. Timbuktu is in *Mali*.

                          KATHY
But the *ancient* capital.

                          STEVE
Yeah. Of *Mali*.

                          LINDSEY
I thought Mali was in the Pacific.

STEVE
(baffled)

In – ?

LINDSEY

Where do they have the shadow puppets?

STEVE
(sputtering)

Are you talking about *Bali?*

KATHY

Same difference.

STEVE

Uhhhh, *no?* The *difference… (cont'd.)*

LINDSEY

And who *gives* a shit, any – ?

(DAN has entered through the kitchen door. Work clothes, mustache, chewing gum. He lingers at a distance.)

STEVE	LINDSEY	LENA
(continuous)	*(continuous)*	I'm sorry. I don't
…is that they	Steve. Steven. It's	mean to interrupt
happen to be *three*	whatever you want	anyone, but –
distinct countries so, I	it to be, okay?	
guess *I* give a shit –		

STEVE
(continuous, lowering his voice, to LINDSEY)

– and could you possibly not talk to me like a *child?*

LENA
(in the clear)

Excuse me?

(All turn to LENA.)

LENA

I was hoping to say something, if I could?

STEVE
(remembering)

Oh oh oh.

TOM

Right.

(to LENA)

Sorry.

(to LINDSEY)

Lena had wanted to mention something and it sounded kind of important so —

KEVIN
(to LENA)

But you don't gotta ask *permission*.

LENA

I'm trying to be polite.

LINDSEY

We're totally rude.

KEVIN

No, you're not.

LINDSEY

It's my family. Irish Catholic, you know? *Blarney.*

KATHY
(raising a hand)

Please, my husband? Half-Jewish half-Italian.

KEVIN

Is that right?

KATHY

Get a word in edgewise.

KEVIN

I believe that.

KATHY

Anyway. Lena.

LENA

Thank you.

LINDSEY

Wait. *Lena,* right?

LENA

Lena.

KATHY

Short for Leonora?

LENA

No.

KATHY

I knew a Leonora.

LENA

It was my aunt's name.

LINDSEY
(reminding herself)

Anyway. Lena, Kevin.

KATHY
(raising hand)

Kathy.

LINDSEY
(indicating)

Kathy, Lindsey, Steve,

STEVE

And Tom.

KEVIN

Don't forget Tom.

LINDSEY

Tom we know. So:

DAN
(from across the room)

Ding-dong?

    (All turn to DAN.)

STEVE

Hey.

DAN

Hey.

STEVE

How's it goin'?

DAN

S'there a Steve anywhere?

STEVE

Yeah?

                                  DAN
You Steve?

                                  STEVE
Yeah?

                                  DAN
Hector said if there's a problem talk to Steve.

                                  STEVE
That's me.

                                  DAN
                            (to the others)
How ya doing?

        TOM   KEVIN   LENA
    Hey. Good.   Doing all right.   Fine, thank you.

                                  DAN
Uhh…

                       (lowers voice, to STEVE)
Quick question?

                                  STEVE
                            (a quiet sidebar)
Yeah?

                                  DAN
So okay. So, we're, uh, digging that trench back there, ya know?

                                  STEVE
Yeah?

                                  DAN
Out in back?

                                STEVE

Yeah?

                                 DAN

For the conduit line?

                                STEVE

Yeah?

                                 DAN

Know what I'm talking about?

                                STEVE

Yeah?

                                 DAN

'Cuz before you hookup that line you gotta bury that conduit?

                                STEVE

Yeah?

                                 DAN

And so in order to dig that trench we gotta take out that tree, right?

                                STEVE

Right?

                                 DAN

Dead tree back there?

                                STEVE

Yeah?

                                 DAN

'Cause those roots, they go down like maybe eight feet?

                                STEVE

Yeah?

                          DAN
Which is why we're taking out that tree?

                          STEVE
Right?

                          DAN
Didja know that thing is *dead?*

                          STEVE
                        (rising)
Hey. Maybe we should –

                        (to the others)
Sorry. You guys go ahead and –

                          DAN
Whoops.

                          STEVE
                        (to DAN)
No no. It's just – two things at once.

                          KEVIN
We can wait.

                          STEVE
No no no. You guys keep –

                        (to DAN)
You wanna show me?

                          DAN
Lemme show ya.

                          STEVE
Lemme take a look.

DAN

Show ya what we're dealing with.

(DAN & STEVE exit out the back door.)

DAN
(overheard to STEVE, as they exit.)
Tell ya one thing though, it is *hot* out here.

(LENA fans herself. A little pause, then:)

LINDSEY

Now I don't remember what we were – ?

TOM

Page three

LINDSEY

Right.

KATHY

Middle of three.

TOM

So. Knowing as we do that the height continues to be the sticking point – and by the way, the reason the petition was drawn up this way in the first place – I mean, nobody wants to be inflexible, but the idea was to set some basic guidelines whereby *if*, say, the height is the problem, like it is here, then one option would be to reduce the total exterior volume, like your husband was saying. And that's the rationale behind the table at the bottom of the page. So what those figures mean, essentially, is that, with each additional foot of elevation beyond the maximum limit, there'd be a corresponding reduction in volume. And the numbers are based on the scale of the *original* structures, which is relatively consistent over the twelve-block radius, and of which this house is a fairly typical example. Now:

ACT II, 2009   131

KATHY

Except we know they're *not.*

TOM

Not what?

KATHY

Not consistent.

TOM

Saying *relatively.*

KATHY

A lotta variables.

TOM

We know that.

KATHY
(beginning a list)
The size of the lots, for starters?

TOM

Right, but –

KATHY

The year of construction?

TOM

Right, so the hope was that, by establishing a couple of regulations up front, hopefully we avoid this kinda situation in the future, 'cause, obviously, it's a pain in the ass for everybody. Now, assuming the Landmarks Committee passes this part of the petition next week –

KATHY

Assuming.

TOM

Safe assumption.

KATHY

And if the Landmarks Committee really wants to pick that fight with the Zoning Department that is *their* business, but that's a matter of *if and when.*

TOM
(to LINDSEY)

Why is this confrontational?

KATHY

Because somebody might've raised these issues when the plans went to the Zoning Department five months ago.

LINDSEY

Kathy.

KATHY

I mean, no one had any objection back *then.*

LINDSEY
(to KEVIN and LENA)

Can I say? We *talked* about renovation. We discussed it. Because these houses are *so* charming and I know it's a shame – but when you figure in the crack in the sub-floor and the cost of the lead abatement – and in a market like this one? It just made more sense to start from scratch.

(TOM's cell rings. He tries to ignore it.)

TOM

Right. *But*: the Owners Association has a vested interest – Kevin and Lena call me up last month, they say Tom, we've got this problem, these people are planning to build a house that's a full fifteen feet taller than all the adjacent structures – *(cont'd.)*

LINDSEY	KATHY
Nooo... *fifteen?* Is that right?	It's exactly what the block is zoned for, Tom.

TOM
(continuous)

– and I think we'd *all* agree that there's a mutual benefit to maintaining the integrity– *(glances at his phone)* – the *architectural* integrity –

LINDSEY

Wanna get that?

TOM

– of a historically significant – god damn it – neighborhood. *(answering)* Yeah?

> *(STEVE returns, as TOM talks on the phone, leaving the kitchen door open.)*

TOM
(into phone)

Yeah, okay, but don't call *me* with that in the middle of a Satur– ? Well, then give it to Marla. Because it's Marla's *account.* Well, where the fuck is Mar– ?
(to the others)
Sorry.

> *(TOM crosses the room to take the call.)*

STEVE

What's happening?

LINDSEY

I don't know.

LENA

You know, it might be a good idea if we all turned off our phones.

LINDSEY

Excellent idea.

KEVIN
(to STEVE)

Get your problem solved?

STEVE

Did what?

KEVIN

Out back.

STEVE

Yeah, I dunno. They hit something.

LINDSEY

What something?

STEVE

I dunno.

LINDSEY

Something dangerous?

STEVE

I dunno.

LINDSEY

Is it going to *explode*?

STEVE

It's not –

(to KEVIN)

– We're putting in a koi pond, and there's a filtration system that has to hook into to the municipal – anyway, they ran into some kind of – whatever. So whatzit, page three?

KEVIN

But maybe wait for Tom?

STEVE
(with a laugh and a shrug)
...standing right *there.*

KEVIN

If we're getting into the legal stuff?

LINDSEY

I agree.

KEVIN

'Cuz, I'm not a lawyer.

STEVE

I'm not a lawyer.

LINDSEY

But, Kathy's a lawyer.

STEVE
(re: TOM)
And he's the one with the time issue.

KEVIN

Long as we're out by four.

STEVE
(okay, but)
It's three-thirty.

KATHY

We'll be done by four.

LINDSEY
(to KEVIN & LENA)
Sorry about all this.

STEVE

Crazy.

(All turn vaguely to TOM, who gestures apologetically and mouths "Sorry." LENA sighs, fans herself.)

KEVIN
(small talk)

When's the baby due?

LINDSEY

Oh. Um, November.

KEVIN

In time for turkey.

LINDSEY

I know.

KEVIN

Boy or girl?

(STEVE is about to answer.)

LINDSEY

No no no. I don't want to know. Ask Steve. Steve saw the ultrasound.
(fingers in ears, eyes closed) La la la la la la la la la la la...

(STEVE mouths the word "boy," then touches LINDSEY's knee.)

LINDSEY
(fingers out of ears, eyes open)

...la la la – either way as long as it's healthy.

KEVIN

Knock wood.

LINDSEY

But something tells me it's a girl.

(Pause. Feet tap. KATHY takes out her phone, dials a number, listens.)

LINDSEY
(to LENA)

You guys have kids?

LENA

Three.

LINDSEY

Wow.

LENA

Mmm.

LINDSEY

How great for you.

LENA

Yes.

LINDSEY

Congratulations.

LENA

Thank you.

(KATHY starts to check messages.)

STEVE
(beat, then to KEVIN)

So Kyle Hendrickson?

KEVIN
(remembering)

Kyle Hendrickson.

STEVE

Kyle Hendrickson – *who,* may I add, kicked my ass in the tenth grade?

Who is this?

KEVIN
(laughing)
Wait wait wait. *Little* Kyle Hendrickson – ?

STEVE
Like the *one* solitary black dude in my entire high school.

KEVIN
Kicked *your* ass?

STEVE
Publicly kicked.

KEVIN
Kyle Hendrickson's like, what? Like five-*two?*

LINDSEY
Wait. *When?*

STEVE
(to KEVIN)
Five-five. J.V. Wrestling team. Tenth grade.

KEVIN
I think that might officially make you – ?

STEVE
A pussy?

KEVIN
Think it might.

LINDSEY
(to STEVE)
Who are you talking about?

STEVE

Okay. Remember I ran into a guy?

LINDSEY

No.

STEVE

Remember last week? I said a guy from middle school?

LINDSEY

No.

STEVE

I was meeting you downtown – oh, and he told me the *joke?*

LINDSEY

Right?

STEVE

The joke I told you?

LINDSEY

I don't remember.

STEVE

The joke about – well, neither do I, at the moment but it was a joke we both thought was funny?

LINDSEY

Okay?

STEVE

Anyway. *That* guy: *That* is Kyle Hendrickson. Who *he* works with.

LINDSEY
(to LENA)

Glad we cleared *that* up.

                              STEVE
Oh oh oh.

                              LINDSEY
What?

                              STEVE
Wait.

                              LINDSEY
What?

                              STEVE
Wait.

                              LINDSEY
What?

                              STEVE
The joke. It's about a guy? Remember? Guy who goes to jail?

                              LINDSEY
No.

                              STEVE
White-collar criminal goes to jail, remember? And and and they put
him in a cell with – ?

                              LINDSEY
                    (realizing, privately to STEVE)
Oh Oh Oh. No.

                              STEVE
What?

                              LINDSEY
Hm-mm.

What?

Let's –

(changing subject, to LENA)

How old are your kids?

STEVE
(to LINDSEY)

Whatsamatter?

KEVIN
(to LINDSEY)

Nine, ten and twelve.

LINDSEY

Wow.

STEVE
(to LINDSEY)

What's your problem?

LINDSEY

Steve.

STEVE

I was telling the joke.

LINDSEY

Later.

STEVE

You said remind me what joke –

LINDSEY

Okay.

STEVE
(laughing)

But now I'm not *allowed* to tell it?

LINDSEY
(quietly)

Stop a second.

STEVE
(to KEVIN)

Anyway. Two guys stuck in a jail cell –

LINDSEY

Steven?

LENA
(finally having had enough)

I'm sorry, and I don't mean to keep interrupting but can somebody please explain to me what it is we're *doing* here?

(Pause. TOM turns. All feel the chill from LENA.)

TOM
(quietly into phone)

Just send me the fucking document.

(KATHY and TOM discreetly hang up.)

LENA

I mean, I know I'm not the only person who takes the situation seriously and I don't like having to be this way but I have been sitting here for the last fifteen minutes waiting for a turn to speak – *(cont'd.)*

(All overlap, quietly chastened.)

TOM	KEVIN	LINDSEY	KATHY
Hey. Sorry 'bout that.	No one's taking *turns*.	I'm so sorry. I really am.	Well, Tom was on the phone, I thought.

LENA
(continuous)

— and meanwhile it seems like nothing is even remotely getting accomplished.

LINDSEY

I agree.

(A truck horn sounds outside.)

KEVIN
(to LENA)

So go ahead and say what you —

LENA
(with a tense smile, to KEVIN)

And could you please not tell me when to — ?

KEVIN

I'm not telling —

LENA
(continuous)

They were having a conversation and — *(cont'd.)*

KEVIN
(overlapping)

And now they stopped.

LENA
(continuous)

— I try not to intrude — *(cont'd.)*

KEVIN

Just being friendly.

LENA
(continous)

– on other peoples' conversations when they're in the middle of them.

(to the others)

I'm not trying to be unfriendly.

LINDSEY

No, it's us.

KEVIN

No it's not.

LINDSEY

No, it is.

KEVIN

You're being friendly.

LENA

I'm being friendly.

LINDSEY
(to KEVIN, re: LENA)

She's being friendly.

STEVE

I'm being friendly.

KEVIN

If anybody's not being friendly –

LENA

Well, maybe the *friendly* thing to do would be for us to respect each other's time, would that be all right?

STEVE	LINDSEY	KATHY	TOM
Yeah. Sure.	*Yes.* Totally.	Was it me? Was it?	Sorry. Really.

LENA

Thank you.

(All murmur quietly.)

STEVE	LINDSEY	KATHY	TOM
(to KEVIN) Was I *disrespectful?*	*So* glad someone has the balls to finally *say* it.	'Cuz, seriously, I thought we'd stopped.	No, you guys? was my fault. That was me.

(Horn sounds again.)

LINDSEY
(to LENA)

Anyway.

LENA

Anyway. All right. *(taking her time)* Well… I have no way of knowing what sort of connection you have to the neighborhood where *you* grew up?

(Horn again. LINDSEY turns to STEVE.)

LINDSEY
(rapid whisper)
Just shut the door. Just shut the fucking —

(STEVE jumps up and exits to shut the kitchen door.)

LINDSEY

Sorry. *(continuing LENA's last line)* The neighborhood where – ?

LENA

And some of our concerns have to do with a particular period
in history and the things that people experienced here in this
community *during* that period —

(*STEVE returns to the circle, sits.*)

STEVE
(*whispering to LENA*)

Sorry.

LENA

— both good and bad, and on a personal level? I just have a lot of
respect for the people who went through those experiences and still
managed to carve out a life for themselves and create a community
despite a whole lot of obstacles?

LINDSEY

As well you should.

LENA

Some of which still exist. That's just a part of my *history* and my
parents' history — and honoring the *connection* to that history — and, no
one, myself included, likes having to dictate what you can or can't
do with your own home, but there's just a lot of *pride,* and a lot of
memories in these houses, and for some of us, that connection still has
value, if that makes any sense?

LINDSEY

Total sense.

LENA

For those of us who have remained.

LINDSEY

Absolutely.

LENA

And *respecting* that memory; that has value, too. At least, that's what *I* believe. And that's what I've been wanting to say.

(All nod solemnly for several seconds at LENA's noble speech.)

STEVE

Um. Can I ask a – ?

LINDSEY
(to STEVE)
Let her finish.

STEVE
(to LENA)
Sorry.

LENA

I was finished.

LINDSEY
(to LENA)

Sorry.

STEVE

Right. So, um… Huh. *(how to say it?)* So, when you use the word *value*, um – ?

LENA

Historical value.

TOM

You read the petition.

STEVE

Yeah.

TOM

Spelled out pretty clearly.

                         STEVE

Right.

                      (to LENA)

But, what I mean is – So, you don't literally mean... *monetary* value. Right?

     (LENA stares.)

                          LENA

My great-aunt –

                         STEVE

Or maybe you do.

                          LENA

– was one of the first people of color to – in a sense, she was a
pioneer –

                         STEVE

No, I understand – and correct me if – but *my* understanding was
that the value of these properties had gone *up*.

                         KATHY

They have.

                         STEVE
                   (to KEVIN & LENA)

Yours included.

                         KEVIN

That's true.

                         STEVE

Way up.

                          TOM

And we'd all like to *keep* it that way.

STEVE

But – You're not suggesting, are you, that, when we build *our* house – ?

(LINDSEY puts a hand on STEVE.)

LINDSEY
(to LENA)

Look, I for one – I am really grateful for what you said, but this is why we sometimes feel defensive, you know? Because we *love* this neighborhood.

STEVE

We do.

LINDSEY

We completely do, and we would never want to to to to carelessly –

STEVE

Run roughshod.

LINDSEY

– over anyone's – And I totally admit, I'm the one who was resistant, especially with the schools and everything, but once I stopped seeing the neighborhood the way it *used* to be, and could see what it is *now*, and its *potential?*

LENA

Used to be what?

LINDSEY

What do you mean?

LENA

What it "used to be"?

STEVE
(helpfully, to LENA)

What *you* said. About the *history* of – ?

LINDSEY

Historically. The changing, you know, demographic – ?

STEVE

Although *originally* –

(to LINDSEY)

– wasn't it German, predominantly?

KATHY

German and Irish.

STEVE

Depending how far back you –

KATHY

It's funny, though. Even though my *father's* family was German, back when *they* were living here –

LINDSEY

Wait, did I know this?

KATHY

I told you that.

LINDSEY

In this neighborhood?

KATHY

(to KEVIN & LENA)

They went to church at St. Stan's! Isn't that crazy?

KEVIN

Is that right?

KATHY

(to KEVIN & LENA)

This is the late fifties. *(laugh)* My father was a "Rotarian"! But my *mother* –

KATHY
(cont'd. to LINDSEY)
She was deaf? I told you that?

LINDSEY   KEVIN
That I knew.   Awwww, that's a shame.

KATHY
(to KEVIN)
Thank you. It was congenital. But then she got pregnant with me and
they moved out to Rosemont, anyway, *her* family, they were *Swedish*.

STEVE
(to KEVIN & LENA)
There was a great article two weeks ago – I don't know if you saw
this – about the history of the changing, uh, ethnic –

LINDSEY   LENA
Distribution.   Oh, I should read that.

STEVE
– of the neighborhood and how in the seventies, eighties, how that
was followed by a period of – of – of – of – of rapid –

KATHY
Decline.

LINDSEY   STEVE   KATHY
No – Not – No   Of *growth*. Of   I don't mean *decline* –
                     growing –

KATHY
– I mean there was *trouble*.

LINDSEY
Not *trouble*, she didn't mean –

152   CLYBOURNE PARK

KEVIN

There was trouble.

LINDSEY

Economic trouble.

KEVIN

Drugs are trouble.

KATHY

That's what I'm saying.

KEVIN

Violence is trouble.

KATHY
(vindicated)

Exactly.

LINDSEY

And the violence as an *outgrowth of* the criminalization of those drugs.

KEVIN
(re: himself and LENA)
'Cuz ya know, the two of us wuz both crackheads.

(A frozen moment, then:)

STEVE	LINDSEY	KATHY	KEVIN
That's funny. I know you're kidding but that *was* the perception at the –	No, come on. Don't say that. Really. Even as a joke.	I know you're joking, but that is exactly what people *thought*.	*(laughs)* I'm kidding you. I'm just messing with you.

STEVE
(to LINDSEY)

– he's *being funny.*

LINDSEY

I know he was, and it *was* funny but when people are systematically *dehumanized* – If you've been placed in some faceless, institutional –

KATHY
(explaining to KEVIN & LENA)

The projects.

LINDSEY

– I mean, like it or not, that kind of environment is not conducive to – to – to – to –

KEVIN

That's true.

LINDSEY

– the formation of *community.*

KATHY

Horrible.

KEVIN

Tough place to grow up.

LINDSEY

With the effect on *children?*

KEVIN

On anyone.

LINDSEY

And to take what had been a pros – well, not prosperous, but a solidly middle-class, um – ?

STEVE

Enclave.

LINDSEY

And then *undermine* the entire economic –

STEVE

Infrastructure.

LINDSEY

– by *warehousing* people inside of these –

STEVE

But that's the thing, right? If you construct some artificial *semblance* of a community, and then isolate people *within* that – I mean, what would be the definition of a *ghetto,* you know? A *ghetto* is a place, Where – *(cont'd.)*

LINDSEY
(overlapping, to STEVE)

But who *uses* that word? I don't.

STEVE
(continuous)

– where, where, where people are *sequestered,* right?

(to LINDSEY, defensively)

The *definition,* I'm saying.

LENA

Well, *my* family –

STEVE

Like Prague. If you think of – *(pedagogically)* Okay: Prague had this ghetto, right? A Jewish ghetto?

LENA
(thanks for the lecture)
We've been to Prague.

LINDSEY
Ohmigod. Prague is *beautiful.* *(KEVIN wiggles his hand)* I loved Pr– you didn't love it?

KEVIN
Prague's *crowded.*

KATHY
And the food sucks. Or is that just me?

STEVE
But I'm saying, It's not like, one day all these Jews were sitting around Prague, looking at the Real Estate section, going, *"Hey here's an idea! Let's all go live in that ghetto!"* Right?

(A beat where they all avoid STEVE's comment. Then:)

LINDSEY
(to LENA)
When were you in Prague?

LENA
Last April.

KEVIN
First Prague, then Zurich.

LINDSEY
I want to go back.

KEVIN
(to STEVE)
You ski?

(A laugh erupts from LINDSEY.)

                          LINDSEY
                      (re: STEVE)

Him?

                           STEVE

You mean – like *downhill?*

                          LINDSEY

That I'd like to see.

                           KEVIN

Ever been to Switzerland?

                           STEVE
                  (to LINDSEY, defensive)

I can *ski.* I *have* skied.

                          LINDSEY

Get that on video.

                           STEVE

Why is that funny?

                          LINDSEY
                (trying not to laugh, to KEVIN)

Sorry.

                           STEVE

Seriously. What is it about the idea of me skiing that you find so
highly, uh – ?

                          LINDSEY

Anyway.

                           STEVE

– *risible?*

KEVIN
(to STEVE)
I just meant, you like to golf, you go to *Scotland*. And if you like to *ski?*

LINDSEY
(still laughing)
Just trying to picture it.

STEVE
Gratuitous.

TOM
(prodding the others)
Annnnnnyway.

LENA	LINDSEY	KATHY
Yes. Maybe we should try to stick to the topic at hand.	Okay. Tom's right Let's get it together.	*(to KEVIN)* I can't ski because I was born with weak ankles. Anyway.

LINDSEY
(to TOM)
Where were we?

TOM
Page three.

LINDSEY
Uggh. You're kidding.

TOM
Nope.

LINDSEY
How can we still be – ?

                              TOM
I dunno.

                              LINDSEY
How is that possible?

                              TOM
                         (glancing at watch)
And it is now... quarter to four.

                              LENA
I'm sorry for taking time.

                              LINDSEY
No. What you said was *great*.

                              LENA
And I wasn't trying to romanticize.

                              LINDSEY
You didn't.

                              LENA
Nothing *romantic* about being poor.

                              LINDSEY
But, it was your *neighborhood*.

                              KATHY
                         (to LENA)
Wait, what street?

                              LENA
Offa Larabee.

                              KATHY
My parents lived on Claremont!

KEVIN

Ya'll would've been neighbors.

LENA

But I didn't mean to make it about my personal *connection* to the house. It's more about the *principle*.

KEVIN

But you can't live in a principle.

LINDSEY

You had a personal connection?

KEVIN

To the house.

LINDSEY

To *this* house?

KEVIN

(to LINDSEY)

Her aunt.

LENA

I don't want to – let's not.

KEVIN

Lived here.

STEVE

Wait. *Who?*

LENA

Sort of beside the point, but yes.

KEVIN

Great-aunt.

LENA

On my mother's side.

LINDSEY

You don't mean, *here*, here?

LENA

And this is fifty years ago.

LINDSEY

Here in this *house*.

LENA

For quite some time, actually.

LINDSEY   STEVE
(hand to her heart)   *Whoa.*
Oh my g–! So so so wait, so – ?

STEVE
(clarifying)

This *exact house*.

LINDSEY
(how weird)
– so, like, you've... *been in this room*?

LENA

I used to climb a tree in the backyard.

LINDSEY   STEVE
Oh my *god*.   Whoa.

LENA

A crepe myrtle tree.

KATHY

Well, that is just bizarre.

KEVIN

Any rate, her great-aunt – and she had to save a long time to be able to afford a house like this.

LENA

She was a domestic worker.

KEVIN

And, a house isn't cheap.

LENA

Not *here*, anyway.

KEVIN

Here at *that* time.

LENA

At *that* time – well, when *I* was growing up I really don't remember seeing a single white face in the neighborhood for pretty much my entire –

KEVIN

Well, one, you said.

LENA

Who?

KEVIN

What's his name?

LENA

Mr. Wheeler?

KEVIN

Mr. Wheeler.

LENA
(to the others)
I don't think anybody knew his first name.

KEVIN

He was a… what?

LENA

(to LINDSEY)

At the grocery store.

KEVIN

Bagged the groceries.

LENA

At the Sup'r – Well, back then it was Gelman's but they tore down Gelman's.

KEVIN

And that became Sup'r Sav'r?

LENA

Well, then they tore down Sup'r Sav'r, so –

KEVIN

You know where the Whole Foods is?

STEVE

And what happened to Mr. Wheeler?

KEVIN

Dead, probably.

LENA

He was, you know… *(taps her temple)*… developmentally… ?

LINDSEY	STEVE	KATHY
Ohhhh. That's so sad.	Huh. Wow. Depressing.	Ohhhh… you know why that upsets me? I have a niece with Asperger's syndrome.

LENA

But, given the makeup of the neighborhood at that time and the
price of a home like this one, the question naturally arises as to
whether it was the thing that happened here in the house – whether
that in some way –

KEVIN

Played a factor.

LENA

In making a place like this affordable. For a person of her income.

(All stare.)

STEVE

The *thing*.

LENA

The sad – you know.

LINDSEY

I don't.

LENA

The tragic –

KEVIN

Thing that happened.

LINDSEY

What thing?

KEVIN
(no big deal)

Well. Long time ago, but –

STEVE

In *this* house?

LENA

I'm just saying that, since she was one of the very first people of color –

LINDSEY

Wait. Something happened in the house?

STEVE

What, somebody *died*, or – ?

KEVIN

S'not important.

LINDSEY

That we should be concerned about?

KEVIN

No no no no no.

LENA

Just that – there'd *been* a family. Who had a son who'd been in the Army.

KEVIN

Korea, maybe?

LENA

And who, well, a few years after he came back from the war –

KEVIN

Killed himself.

LINDSEY
(beat)

Oh my god.

KEVIN

Yeah.

STEVE

Wow.

Oh my god.

Sad.

Wow.

Oh my god.

Which my great-aunt didn't know at the time.

Oh my god, that is just –

Though I assumed you *did*.

Umm, no?

That is just – just – just – Wait. And they went ahead and *sold* the house to – ?

Mm-hmm.

Wow.

Without *telling* her that? Because nobody ever told *us* that.

Well, they *wouldn't*, would they?

KEVIN
(dismissive)

Fifty *years* ago.

LINDSEY
(to KATHY)

But *legally,* I mean, don't you have to *tell* people that?

KATHY

Not if you want to sell it.

LENA

It was something like he'd come back from the Army. And he'd been
accused of something.

KEVIN

Killing people.

LENA

Innocent people.

KEVIN

Killing civilians.

STEVE

But you don't mean, like like like like… *(laughs)* like *here in this very –* ?

LENA

No – I mean, not *where we're sitting.*

KEVIN

Upstairs, wasn't it?

LINDSEY
(freaking out)

I – I – I – I –

STEVE
(touching LINDSEY)

Breathe.

LINDSEY
(pushing STEVE'S hand away)

Stop it.

LENA

I mean, the version *I* was told was, that he went upstairs.

KEVIN

Hanged himself.

LINDSEY
(standing, walking away)

Okay. *No.* No, I'm sorry, but that is *wrong.*

STEVE
(following her)

Where are you going?

LINDSEY

That is just – *No.* To sell someone a – a – a *house,* where – ?

STEVE

Whatsamatter?

(STEVE and LINDSEY exit to the kitchen, from where we clearly hear:)

LINDSEY

No. There should be a *law.* And I don't care *how,* okay? I don't want to know *how* he did it or in *what room* – Because I'm sorry, but that is just something that, from a legal standpoint, you should have to *tell* people!

KATHY
(calling to LINDSAY)

It's not.

LINDSEY
(sticking her head in, to KATHY)
Well, it fucking well should be.

STEVE

Hey. Hey.

LINDSEY
(privately, to STEVE)
And now I have this horrifying *image* in my head?

STEVE
(to LINDSEY, laughing)
But why d'you have to make such a big *deal* outa – ?

LINDSEY
Uh, it *is* a big deal, Steve. If your *child* – if *our family* is going to *live* in a house where – ?

STEVE
(laughing, to the others)
I mean, it's not like he's still *hanging* up there!

LINDSEY
(losing her shit, to STEVE)
It's not *funny, okay?!!* *It's not funny to me, so why are you acting like an asshole?!!*

(The kitchen door bangs open and DAN noisily enters.)

DAN
(calling out)
Okay. Show ya whatcha got.

(He drags a large trunk – the same trunk we saw in Act I, now covered with mold and dirt – into the middle of the room.)

DAN

So that's your problem right there. *(coughs a couple of times)* 'Scuse me. And I tell ya one thing: Yank this up from down there, take a look at it, you know the first thing I'm thinking to myself? You know what I'm thinking? *Buried treasure.* Like Spanish doubloons or something and I know you're thinking Dan ya crazy bastard but I tell ya what. I know a guy.

(He joins the circle.)

DAN
(coughs again)

'Scuse me. This guy. Last summer he's taking out a septic system – this house out in Mundelein. He's sitting on top of his backhoe. All of a sudden *clang*. And this guy's not exactly the sharpest tool in the box, if ya know what I mean, but he goes down in there about five, six feet with a chain and a winch – swear to god – ya know what he pulls out from down there? He stands back. He takes a look – *(without stopping)* – You're in the middle of something.

STEVE

Sorta.

DAN

My bad.

STEVE

No no.

DAN

Bull in a china shop.

STEVE

It's cool.

                              DAN
According to my wife.

                              STEVE
Oh yeah?

                              DAN
As well as a couple other names not suitable for mixed – Anyways.

                              STEVE
Thanks.

                              DAN
                         (re: the trunk)
So, I'll just leave this here for ya.

                              STEVE
Thank you.

                              DAN
Need me to open it, you lemme know.

                              STEVE
Great.

                              DAN
Problem, though. *(indicating the large padlock)* Problem's this puppy
right here. Now the deal is: I got a saw. Take a hacksaw you could
maybe saw it off but whatcha really want is a pair of bolt cutters and
I don't think I got any bolt cutters, so.

                              STEVE
Ah, well.

                              DAN
'Cause you never know. Turns out to be fulla Spanish doubloons we'll
haveta split it six ways, huh?

(to DAN, taking over)

Sorry.

DAN

Whoops.

LINDSEY

I don't know your name.

DAN
(extending hand)

Dan.

LINDSEY

Hi Dan.

DAN

Dan or Danny.

LINDSEY

Great.

DAN

Daniel when the wife gets pissed.

LINDSEY

But listen –

DAN

No no no no no no I gotcha.

LINDSEY

If you wouldn't mind?

DAN

Middle of your thing and I come barging right into –

LINDSEY

Thank you.

DAN

But you findya some bolt cutters you'll be in business.

LINDSEY

We will.

DAN
(an idea)

Hey, ya know what? Hang on a second.

(DAN heads to the back door. As he does:)

TOM

So I'm just going to push ahead, if that's okay?

DAN
(calling out the door, top of his lungs)

Ramirez!!!

TOM

'Cause we still got seventeen pages to cover –

LINDSEY
(to all)

And I'm sorry I lost my shit. No, I did. But I think we're both wound
a little tight right now with the baby and the house and the money
and everything –

DAN
(same)

Ramirez!!

LINDSEY

– and then to top it all off, we get sent this petition in the mail, you
know, and suddenly our entire lives are thrown into chaos at the very

same moment that – I mean, the demolition was scheduled to start on Monday and unless we get this resolved which I want as much as anyone then what do people expect?

DAN

Ram–!!! Ah, screw it.

(DAN gives up, exits.)

TOM
(continuing)
So: Couple of options. One, as we said, is reducing the height –

KATHY
(adamantly)
No. Tom, I'm sorry, but you can't just call an architect at the eleventh hour and snap your fingers and say can you completely redesign an entire –

LINDSEY
It's a little late in the day for that.

LENA
(to LINDSEY)
I'm sorry you're upset.

LINDSEY
I'm not upset. I'm not.

KATHY
And may I remind everybody that these guys are under no obligation, legal *or* otherwise –

TOM
(holding up a document)
Okay. Here's the wording from the City Council, and I quote: "In recognition of the *historic* status of the Clybourne Park neighborhood, and its distinctive collection of *low-rise single-family homes — (cont'd.)*

LINDSEY	KEVIN	TOM
Aren't *we* a single family?	Hey. Hey. Everything's cool.	*(continuous)* *— intended to house a community of working-class families."*

LINDSEY
And you know, the thing is? Communities change.

STEVE
They do.

LINDSEY
That's just the reality.

STEVE
It is.

LENA
And some change is inevitable, and we all support that, but it might be worth asking yourself who exactly is *responsible* that change?

(Little pause.)

LINDSEY	KEVIN
I'm not sure what you – ?	Wait, what are you trying to – ?

LENA
I'm asking you to think about the motivation behind the long-range political initiative to change the face of this neighborhood.

(Another little pause.)

LINDSEY	STEVE	KEVIN
What does that mean? I don't know what that – ?	*(to LENA)* Wait, say that again?	The long-range *what?*

LENA

I mean that this is a highly desirable area.

STEVE

Well, *we* desire it.

LENA

I know you do.

LINDSEY

Same as you.

LENA

And now the area is *changing*.

KATHY

And for the *better*, right?

LENA

And I'm saying that there are certain economic interests that are being served by those changes and others that are not. That's all.

STEVE
(suspiciously)

And… *which* interests are being – ?

LENA
(systematically)

If you have a residential area, in direct proximity to *downtown*?

STEVE

Right?

LENA

And if that area is occupied by a particular *group*?

STEVE

Which group?

LINDSEY

(to LENA)

You know what? We're talking about *one house*.

LENA

(to LINDSEY)

I understand that.

STEVE

Which group?

LINDSEY

A house for our *family*?

STEVE

Which group?

LENA

That's how it happens.

LINDSEY

In which to raise our *child*?

STEVE

No no. Which group?

LENA

It happens one house at a time.

STEVE

Whoa whoa whoa. Okay. Stop right there.

LINDSEY

What are you doing?

No. I'm sorry, but can we just come out and *say* what it is we're actually – ? Shouldn't we maybe *do* that? Because if *that's* what this is really about, then… jesus, maybe we oughta save ourselves some time and and and and just… *say* what it is we're really *saying* instead of doing this elaborate little *dance* around it.

> *(Dead stop. All stare at STEVE.)*

STEVE

Never mind.

KATHY

What dance?

STEVE

I – I – I – I shouldn't have – whatever.

LENA
(parsing his meaning)
So… you think I haven't been *saying* what I *actually* – ?

STEVE
(laughs)
Uhhh… Not to my way of thinking, no.

LENA

Well, what is it you *think* I'm – ?

STEVE

I – I – I… *(laughs incredulously)* …like we don't all know?

LINDSEY

I don't.

STEVE

Oh, *yes you do*. Of *course* you do.

KEVIN

Well, maybe you oughta *tell* us what *you* think she was saying.

STEVE

Oh oh, but it has to be *me?*

LENA

Well, you're the one who raised the question as to – *(cont'd.)*

STEVE
(laughs, overlapping)

Oh, *come on.* It was *blatant.*

LENA
(continuous)

– the sincerity of my speech.

LINDSEY

What the fuck, Steve?

STEVE

You know what? Forget I said it.

LINDSEY	LENA	STEVE
You didn't *say* anything.	Oh no, I'm *interested.*	Let's forget the whole –

STEVE
(continuous)

– Okay. Okay. If you really want to – It's... *(tries to laugh, then, sotto)*
...it's *race.* Isn't it? You're trying to tell me that that... That implicit
in what you *said* – That this entire conversation... isn't at least *partly*
informed – *am I right? (laughs nervously)* By the issue of... *(sotto)* of
racism?

(Beat, then:)

LINDSEY   STEVE

(to STEVE)   *(to LINDSEY)*

Are you out of your – ?   And *please* don't do that to me, okay? I've asked you repeatedly.

(to LENA)

I have no idea where this is coming from.

LENA

Well, the *original* issue was the inappropriately large *house* that – *(cont'd.)*

STEVE

(to LENA, overlapping)

Oh, come *on.*

LENA

(continuous)

– you're planning to build. Only, *now* I'm fairly certain that I've been called a *racist.*

STEVE

But I didn't say that, did I?

LENA

Sounded like you did.

STEVE

(to KEVIN)

Did I say that?

KEVIN

Yeah, you kinda did.

STEVE

In what way did I say that?

KEVIN

Uh, *somebody* said racism.

-Cism! -Cism! Not *-cist!!*

KEVIN

Which must originate from *somewhere.*

STEVE

And which we all find totally reprehesnsi–

KEVIN

So – are *you* the racist?

STEVE

Can I just – ?

KEVIN

Is it your wife?

KATHY

Don't look at *me.*

STEVE

Look:

KEVIN

'Cause, by process of elimination –

STEVE

Here's what I'm saying:

LINDSEY

What *are* you saying?!

STEVE

I'm saying: Was race *not* a factor –

LINDSEY
(re: STEVE, exonerating herself)
I don't know this person.

Were there *not* these differences –

What differences!!? There's no –

STEVE
(to LINDSEY re: LENA)
Okay: She walks in here, from the very beginning, with all these *issues* – *(cont'd.)*

LENA
(overlapping)
About your *house*.

STEVE
(continuous)
– and I'm only asking whether, were we not, shall we say – ?

LINDSEY
You're *creating* an issue. *Where none exists.*

STEVE
Oh oh oh you *heard* what she *said*. She as much as claimed that there's some kind of, of, of *secret conspiracy* –

LENA
Oh, it's not a *secret*.

KEVIN	LENA	STEVE
(to LENA)	*(to KEVIN)*	There. Thank you.
Ohh, *c'mon*. Are you	Oh, please don't be	*Now you see what*
seriously – ?	purposely *naive*.	*I'm* – ?

LENA
This has been under discussion for at least *four decades* now – *(cont'd.)*

KEVIN
(overlapping, to LENA)

You can't prove that.

LENA
(continuous)
– at the highest institutional levels of –

(to KEVIN)
– oh, don't act like you don't know it's true.

STEVE
(to LENA)
What, and now we're the evil invaders who are –

LINDSEY
(to STEVE)

She never said that!!!!

STEVE
– appropriating your *ancestral homeland?*

LINDSEY
(to STEVE)
This, this, this – No. I'm sorry, this is the most *asinine* –

(to LENA and KEVIN)
Half of my friends are black!

STEVE
(sputtering)

What!!??

LINDSEY
(to STEVE, as to a child)
As is true for most *normal* people.

Name *one*.

LINDSEY

Normal people? Tend to have *many* friends of a diverse and wide-ranging –

STEVE

You can't name *one!*

LINDSEY

Candace.

STEVE
(beat, then)

Name another.

LINDSEY

I don't have to stand here compiling a list of –

STEVE

You said *half*. You *specifically –*

LINDSEY

Theresa.

STEVE

She works in your office!! She's not your "friend".

LINDSEY

She was at the baby shower, Steve! I hope she's not my enemy!!

TOM

Well, this is all fascinating –

STEVE
(to LINDSEY)

Name another.

TOM

And while I'd love to sit here and review *all* of American History, *maybe* we should concentrate on the plans for your *property* – *(cont'd.)*

STEVE
(overlapping)

Yes!! Yes!! *(cont'd.)*

TOM
(continuous)

– which *had* been the *original* topic of the convers–

STEVE
(overlapping, continuous)

The history of America *is* the history of private property.

LENA

That may be –

STEVE

Read De Tocqueville.

LENA

– though I rather doubt *your* grandparents were *sold as* private property.

STEVE
(to KEVIN & LENA)

Ohhhhh my *god*. Look. Look. Humans are *territorial*, okay?

LINDSEY
(to STEVE)

Who *are* you?

STEVE

This is why we have *wars*. One group, one *tribe*, tries to usurp some *territory* – and now *you guys* have *this* territory, right? And you don't like having it *stolen away* from you, the way white people stole everything else from black America. *We get it,* okay? And we *apologize.* But what *good* does it do, if we perpetually fall into the same, predictable little euphemistic tap dance around the topic?

KEVIN

You know how to tap dance?

STEVE

See? See what he's doing?!!

LINDSEY

Maybe quit while you're ahead.

STEVE

No. I'm sick of — *No.* Every *single word* we say is — is — is *scrutinized* for some kind of latent — Meanwhile you guys run around saying n-word this and n-word that and *whatever.* We all know *why* there's a double standard but I can't even so much as repeat a fucking *joke* that *the one black guy I know told me —*

KEVIN

So tell the goddamn joke.

STEVE

Not *now!!*

KEVIN

If you feel so *oppressed,* either go ahead and *tell it —*

LINDSEY
(to STEVE)

Do *not.*

KEVIN

— or maybe you could *move on.*

LINDSEY
(with finality)

Thank you!

LENA

Well, I want to hear it.

KEVIN

(to LENA)

Ohh, *don't.*

LENA

(to KEVIN)

Why not? You're not interested?

LINDSEY

No. Trust me. It's offensive.

STEVE

(to LINDSEY)

Of course it's *offensive* — *(cont'd.)*

LINDSEY

(overlapping)

To *me.* Offensive to *me.*

STEVE

(continuous)

— that's the whole point of the — How? How does it offend *you?*

LINDSEY

Because it's disgusting and juvenile and traffics in the worst possible type of obsolete bullshit stereotypes.

LENA

Well, now I *gotta* hear it.

KEVIN

No no no no no. Aww, *c'mon.*

STEVE

No. I can't.

LINDSEY

Not while I'm in the room.

LENA

(to KEVIN, re: LINDSEY)

Well, she says it's so offensive, and I have no way of knowing if she's right, and if I don't ever *hear* it, how will I ever *know?*

(KEVIN sighs, throws up his hands.)

                          STEVE

Um, you know what? I don't even remember it now.

                          LENA

Two men in jail, you said.

                          KATHY

Oh, *I* know this one!

                          LINDSEY
                      (a warning)

Steven?

                          LENA

Wasn't that it? Two men...?

                          STEVE

I – Okay. So there's – *Look, it's not even my joke, okay?!!* It was told to me by Kyle Hendrickson, who, for what it's worth, happens to be –

                          LENA

Black.

                          STEVE

Right.

                          LENA

So the white man goes to jail.

                          LINDSEY
                      (to STEVE)

I can't believe you actually intend to – !! Fine.

                          STEVE

Anyway.

                          LINDSEY

Knock 'em dead.

                           STEVE
Goes to jail for… you know. Embezzlement. Something. Little white
guy. And he's put in a jail cell with this… uhhh…

                           LENA
With a black man.

                           STEVE
Big black guy.

                           LINDSEY
                        (appalled)
And why *"big"*? *(cont'd.)*

                           STEVE
                 (overlapping, to LINDSEY)
I am repeating, *verbatim*, a joke – *(cont'd.)*

                           LINDSEY
                        (continuous)
Why does it have to be "big"? What does that reveal about your
subconscious – ?

                           STEVE
                        (conitinuous)
– in the precise manner in which it was told to *me*.

                           LENA
Little white man.

                           LINDSEY
                       (head in hands)
Oh god.

                           LENA
Big black man.

In the… yeah, so they… um, slam the cell door… behind him, I guess, and the black guy turns to the white guy, black guy goes, "Okay, I'm gonna give you a choice. While you're in here with me, you can either be the mommy, or you can be the daddy." And the white guy thinks for a second and he goes, "Uh, well, um, I guess, if it's up to *me*, then, I guess I'd have to say *I'd* prefer to be the daddy." *(clears his throat)* And, the black guy goes, "Okay, well then bend over 'cause Mommy's gonna fuck you in the ass."

(Long pause. No one laughs or smiles. They simply nod or shake their heads. Finally…)

KATHY

That's not the one I was thinking of.

STEVE
(academically)

So: Is that "*offensive*"?

LENA   LINDSEY

No.   *Are you ins– ?!?!!!*

STEVE
(to LINDSEY)

To *you.* How is it offensive to *you?*

LINDSEY

I don't think it's *me* you should be *asking.*

LENA

No, the problem with *that* joke, see, is that it's not *funny.*

LINDSEY

No shit.

STEVE
(to LINDSEY)
You laughed when I told it to you!!

LENA
And had it been a *funny* joke –

STEVE
It *is* funny. Yes it is. And and and and the *reason* it's funny, is, is, is that it plays upon certain latent fears of – of – of – of white people, vis-a-vis the –

TOM
Okay. I'd like to add: I'm *gay*.

STEVE	KATHY	LINDSEY
I – I – I – I – well, I didn't know that.	See? You never know. You really don't.	Nice. Nice going, Steven. Nice work.

(to TOM)
I couldn't tell at *all*.

TOM
So I guess you think sex *between men* is funny

STEVE
Oh, come on!!!

TOM
Just *inherently* funny.

STEVE
And it's not even *sex*, it's *rape!*

LINDSEY
So *rape* is funny.

STEVE

N– *Yes!!!* In the context of the *joke.*

KATHY

My sister was raped.

STEVE

I quit.

KATHY

So it's offensive to *me.*

LINDSEY

And me!

STEVE
(re: TOM)

And him. *And* them. *That's the point of the joke.* To permit the expression of – And what does it even *mean,* "Offended"? I don't even know what it *means.*

KEVIN

How many white men does it take to change a light bulb?

TOM	LINDSEY	KATHY	STEVE
Okay, I'm about two minutes from leaving? So, *heads up.*	No. Can we please *not?* I'm asking you as a favor.	Aha. See? Shoe's on the other foot now.	*Fine!* Tell me the joke. I want to hear it. I do. *(cont'd.)*

STEVE
(continuous)

How many white men *does* it take to change a light bulb?

KEVIN

All of 'em.

STEVE

And why is that?

KEVIN

One to hold the light bulb while the rest of 'em screw the entire world.

STEVE

So?!! You think I'm *"offended"?* I can do this all day. What's long and hard on a black man?

LINDSEY

How is this happening?!!

KEVIN

I don't know, Steve. What *is* long and hard on a black man?

STEVE

First grade. Are you "offended"?

KEVIN

Nope.

STEVE

Neither am I.

LINDSEY

You *can't be* offended, you *moron — (cont'd.)*

STEVE
(astonished laugh)

...I *can't?*

LINDSEY
(continuous)

— because you've *never* been politically marginalized, unlike *the majority* of people in the world — *(cont'd.)*

STEVE
(overlapping)

How can a *majority* be *marginal?*

LINDSEY
(continuous)

– and, by the way, *all women, everywhere*, and it's your classic white male
myopia that you're blind to that basic fact.

LENA

Why is a white woman like a tampon?

(All turn to LENA. Pause.)

LINDSEY

Why is what?

LENA

It's a joke.

KEVIN

No no no no no no –

LENA

You told a joke, now *I'm* telling one: Why is a white woman – *(cont'd.)*

KEVIN
(overlapping)

Baby, don't.

LENA
(privately, continuous to KEVIN)

– and please don't *baby* me. You've got three babies at *home* – *(cont'd.)*

KEVIN
(publicly, overlapping)

Good night. I wash my hands.

LENA
(continuous)

– if you need to *pacify* someone.

(to the others)

So:

STEVE
(raising a finger)

Uhh... can you repeat the setup?

LENA

Why...

STEVE

...is a white woman, right...?

LENA

...like a tampon?

(STEVE looks around. No one else answers, so:)

STEVE

Um, I don't know, why?

LENA

Because they're both stuck up cunts.

(Pause. Again, no one laughs or smiles. KEVIN shakes his head.)

LINDSEY
(even)

Wow.

LENA

But I hope you're not *offended.*

STEVE
(academically, <u>not</u> laughing)

See, *I* find that funny.

LINDSEY

Do you.

KATHY

Well, *I'm* offended.

STEVE

Oh, you are not.

LINDSEY

And how does it always comes back around to *the women*?

LENA
(innocently)

It was just a joke.

STEVE

Exactly!!

KATHY

An extremely *hostile* joke.

LINDSEY

Directed at me.

KATHY

And in what way am I *stuck up*, exactly? You mean, because I worked my ass off putting myself through law school, that makes me *stuck up?*

STEVE

It's a joke about a *tampon!!*

KATHY

And maybe there's a difference between being *stuck up* and being *intelligent.*

STEVE

(to KATHY)
You don't even know the fucking capital ofMorocco!!!

KATHY

(insulted)

Ohhhhhhh...kay.

STEVE

And you know something? If there's anyone here who's being *marginalized* by the tide of history – You don't exactly see *me* sitting in the White House, do you?

LINDSEY

Thank the Lord.

STEVE

But you don't see *me* wetting my pants and acting all "offended".

KATHY

(to LINDSEY, as she packs her things.)
You know, I think maybe I'm *done.*

STEVE

No. You want to know what offends *me?* How about the neighborhood the two of us are living in right now? Bunch of white suburban assholes still driving around with the yellow ribbon magnets on their SUVs in support of some bullshit war. *That's* the kinda shit that offends *me.*

KEVIN

Why does *that* make them assholes

(STEVE stares at KEVIN.)

STEVE

Why does what?

Said assholes have yellow ribbons on their SU—

STEVE

I didn't say that.

KEVIN

Yeah, you did, you said —

STEVE

I said *"with"* the magnet, not, you know, *"by virtue of"*.

KEVIN

So, it's not the *magnet* makes you the asshole?

LINDSEY
(to KEVIN)

You have one on your car?

KEVIN

I have three of 'em.

STEVE

Three.

KEVIN

Three.

LINDSEY

Three?

LENA

Three.

STEVE

Three.

KEVIN

One for each member of my family serving overseas.

                              STEVE
Great.

        (Beat.)

                              KATHY
I have the pink one for breast cancer.

                              KEVIN
So maybe I'm a *triple* asshole, but —

                              LINDSEY
                    (fake-whisper to KEVIN)
I think we know who the asshole is.

                              STEVE
Wow.

                              LINDSEY
                    (finishing off STEVE)
Well you're being an *idiot*. And in case you hadn't noticed, the rest
of the world has begun a more sophisticated conversation about
this topic than you apparently are qualified to participate in at this
incredible moment in history. I mean, I used to *date* a black guy. *So
what?* I mean, *seriously. Steve. Wake up.*

        *(The same church bell that we heard in Act I begins to ring. Pause.
        TOM looks at his watch.)*

                              TOM
                    (claps hands together)
And it is now four o'clock.

                              STEVE
                    (privately, to LINDSEY)
When did you date a black guy?

So: Final thoughts? Lena?

No.

TOM
Kev?

KEVIN
I'm good.

TOM
Anybody?

KEVIN
Very informative.

LINDSEY
Well, I want to say this: I want to say I feel angry. And I'm basically
kind of hurt by the implication that's been made that, just because we
want to live as your neighbors and raise a child alongside yours, that
somehow, in the process of doing that, we've had our ethics called
into question. Because *that* is hurtful.

LENA
(calmly)
No one has questioned your *ethics* at all.

LINDSEY
Well, I wish I could believe you.

LENA
No, what we're questioning is your *taste*.

(The others rise to leave.)

<table>
<tr><td>

TOM

Kathy? I will call you when the
petition goes through.

</td><td>

LINDSEY

Well, *that* was insulting.

</td></tr>
</table>

KATHY

Thank you.

TOM

Tuesday at the latest.

LINDSEY

Wait, what's wrong with our *taste?*

TOM
(putting on sunglasses)

Kev?

KEVIN

Right behind you.

LINDSEY

No. What is so *egregious* about the design of our *house?*

KEVIN
(to LENA, who is about to respond)

No no no no no. Let it go.

(LENA exits.)

KATHY
(to LINDSEY)

Sweetie, I've got a thing but I'll call you tomorrow.

TOM
(to LINDSEY and STEVE)

And you guys got my number if you want to talk?

Yep.

(TOM is gone, with a thumbs-up. KATHY follows close behind. At the same time, DAN enters from the kitchen carrying a pair of bolt cutters. The others ignore him.)

KEVIN
(to LINDSEY and STEVE)
So, uhh… good luck with your house. And maybe ya'll can just communicate with Tom from here on out. But, anyway, uhh… *(with a wave)* …ya'll enjoy the rest of your evening.

(KEVIN politely exit through the open front door. STEVE and LINDSEY sit silently for a moment, then:)

DAN
(holding up the bolt cutters)
Uhhhhh…?

LINDSEY
(quietly)
Wow.

STEVE
Wow is right.

LINDSEY
Amazing.

STEVE
(but not quietly enough)
And for the record? *That woman* is the cunt.

(And instantly KEVIN is back through the front door.)

KEVIN
(advancing on STEVE)
Wait a second – *what'd* you say?

(All hell breaks loose.)

LENA	KEVIN	STEVE	LINDSEY
(following KEVIN) Just leave it alone. Let 'em be. I don't care what kinda bullshit they think, all I want to do is go home and now and take the longest shower of my life.	Whattya think I'm *deaf* or something? Standing right there on your front doorstep – Oh no, I *heard* you loud and clear. I'm just giving you the opportunity to repeat it to my *face*... *(cont'd.)*	*(innocently)* What? What? What? I didn't... Hey, hey, hey, *whoa. Back off,* man. What is your fucking problem, dude? I didn't do anything to you *or* to her so why can't you *chill*?	*(to KEVIN)* No no no no – I told you. It's the pressure. We're both under a huge amount of pressure and yes he acted like an idiot but could we all just maybe *step off,* please?

KEVIN
(continuous, in the clear)
...and when you do? I will slap the taste outa your mouth.

STEVE
Oh oh oh good, *threaten me.*

LENA
Oh, *now* you're gonna stand up for me?

KEVIN
Don't you ever insult my wife, you hear me, *bitch*

DAN
(putting his hand on KEVIN's shoulder)
Hey. Let's be civilized.

KEVIN
(whirling on DAN)
Ohoho, don't you touch *me*.

DAN	STEVE	KEVIN	LENA
Whoa whoa whoa. That's cool. I'm just passing through, is all.	*(to DAN)* Hey, do you *mind*, okay? We happen to be having a conversation.	*(to DAN)* Go putting your hands on *me?* Oh, no. Not in *this* neighbor–	*(to KEVIN)* Oh, for god's sake, are you coming –

LENA
(continuous)
– or are you too busy trying to make *friends* with everybody?

(DAN backs off as two simultaneous arguments unfold.)

LINDSEY
(to STEVE)
And why the fuck did you go and insult Kathy? We are *paying* her, I hope you realize?

STEVE
Yeah, well you know what? I *agree* with them! *The house is too fucking big!*

LINDSEY
Ohhhhhhhhhhhh do not *even* –

KEVIN
(to LENA)
What the hell is that supposed to – ?

LENA
Alllllllllll afternoon. Always gotta be *every*-body's friend. *Hi everybody! I'm Kevin!*

KEVIN
(starting to exit)
Oh gimme a fuckin' – So you want to fight with *me* now? Gotta pick a fight with *me?*

<table>
<tr><td>

STEVE
Very first time we saw the plans.
What did I tell you? I told you
that like fifteen times!!

</td><td>

KEVIN
(cont'd.)
You have had a bug up your ass
from the moment we walked
through this door.

</td></tr>
<tr><td>

LINDSEY
Well, Steven, you're free to live
whereever you want, but the
baby and I will be here if you
ever feel like visiting.

</td><td>

LENA
Yeah, well maybe some of
us don't feel the need to
constantly *ingratiate* ourselves
with everybody.

</td></tr>
<tr><td></td><td>

KEVIN
Well, maybe that's because some
of us aren't *paranoid* and *delusional*.

</td></tr>
</table>

(KEVIN and LENA exit. By this point, DAN has succeeded in opening the trunk. STEVE and LINDSEY fold chairs and gather their things as they bicker.)

STEVE
(continuous from above)
Fine by me.

LINDSEY
Do you have the keys?

STEVE
I mean, God forbid my needs should ever come before the *baby's*.

LINDSEY
You really want me to choose between you and the baby?

STEVE
Oh, I'm secondary.

LINDSEY
Cause that's an *easy* one.

STEVE

Correction: *Tertiary.*

*(As LINDSEY & STEVE continue to argue, a bespectacled
young man in a military uniform descends the stairs, unnoticed and
oddly out of place. This is KENNETH, played by the actor who
played TOM. He carries a yellow legal pad and a transistor radio.
Oblivious to the scene around him, he takes a seat by a window near
the front door. DAN removes a yellowed envelope from the trunk as
LINDSEY and STEVE prepare to leave.)*

LINDSEY

Or maybe you don't *want* the baby.

STEVE

Oh! That's funny. I didn't know I had a *choice.*

LINDSEY

Oh, you had a choice.

STEVE

If only I'd *known.*

LINDSEY

And you *chose.*

STEVE

And what were the options, again? Oh that's right. A) *Let's have a baby.*

LINDSEY

Which you *chose.*

STEVE

Or B) *I'm divorcing you.*

LINDSEY

But *you* chose *A.*

                    STEVE
A for Arm-twisting.

                    LINDSEY
Do you have the keys?

                    STEVE
B for *Blackmail.*

                    LINDSEY
                (from outside)
Do you have them or don't – ?

                    STEVE
                (from the door)
YES! YES I HAVE THE GODDAMN – What, you think
someone's gonna *rob* this place?

        (DAN turns to see them exit.)

                    STEVE
Help yourselves. Fuckin' shithole.

        *(STEVE slams the door. DAN looks around with no
        acknowledgment of KENNETH.)*

                    DAN
                (to the empty house)
Hello? *(beat)* Hello?

        (He sits on the trunk, opens the letter.)

                    DAN
                (reading to himself)
Dear Mom and Dad.

                    BEV
                (bleary-eyed, confused)
Kenneth?

        (KENNETH turns down the volume on the radio.)

KENNETH
Hmm?

BEV

What are you doing down here?

KENNETH

Writing a letter.

BEV

Oh. *(beat)* Did your father leave already?

KENNETH
(looks outside)

I don't see the car.

BEV

What time is it?

KENNETH

Don't know.

BEV

I overslept.

KENNETH

Yup.

BEV
(yawning)

I don't know why I was up so late. I was up half the night and the house was so quiet and your father was sound asleep but for some reason my mind was just racing and it took forever to fall asleep.

KENNETH

Go back to bed.

                    BEV
              (finally focusing)
Oh look how you're dressed up. Why are you all dressed up like that?

        (KENNETH stares, doesn't answer.)

                    BEV
Kenneth?

                  KENNETH
Job interview.

        *(A key turns in the front door. It opens and FRANCINE enters in
        her street clothes with a scarf tied around her head. She carries a wet
        umbrella.)*

                  FRANCINE
                  (sleepy)
Morning.

                  KENNETH
Morning.

                    BEV
Morning, Francine.

                  FRANCINE
Morning.

                    BEV
Oh, is it *raining* out there?

                  FRANCINE
Sprinkling a little.

                    BEV
I didn't even notice. Well. It's good for the grass.

(She stands at the bottom of the stairs, as FRANCINE crosses past her and up the hallway. BEV lingers on the stairs.)

KENNETH

Aren't you going back to sleep?

BEV
(pensive)

Oh, I will. I'm just about to. But you know, I think things are about to change. I really do. I know it's been a hard couple of years for all of us, I know they have been, but I really believe things are about to change for the better. I firmly believe that.

(KENNETH waits. BEV turns and starts back up the stairs.)

BEV

You have enough light, there?

KENNETH

Uh-huh.

BEV
(as she ascends)

Well, don't hurt your eyes.

(She is gone. KENNETH turns the radio back up, resumes writing. DAN continues to read. The lights slowly fade as the music concludes.)

End of play.